# ONE WEEK LONG

Jane Ward

© 2007 National Institute of Adult Continuing Education
(England and Wales)

21 De Montfort Street
Leicester LE1 7GE
Company registration no. 2603322
Charity registration no. 1002775

NIACE has a broad remit to promote lifelong learning
opportunities for adults. NIACE works to develop increased
participation in education and training, particularly for those
who do not have easy access because of class, gender, age,
race, language and culture, learning difficulties or
disabilities, or insufficient financial resources.

For a full catalogue of all NIACE's publications visit
**www.niace.org.uk/publications**

Cataloguing in Publications Data

A CIP record for this title is available from the British Library

ISBN 978-1-86201-322-3

Designed and typeset by Boldface Typesetters, London
Printed and bound by Ashford Colour Press, Gosport

# Contents

# Acknowledgements

Among the pleasures of writing this book were the many dialogues and debates about ESOL with colleagues which were always informative, interesting and challenging. I would like to thank everyone who gave their time to exchange ideas, point me to sources, read drafts and offer helpful comments and suggestions. Particular thanks are due to the chair of the NIACE ESOL Committee of Inquiry, Derek Grover, the members, Mary Alys, Jenny Burnette, Mary Clayton, Mary Coussey, Sue Diplock, Paul Hambley, Paul Head, Ursula Howard, Denia Kincade, Jane Luff, Jackie McLoughlin, Alastair Pearson, Helen Sunderland, John Taylor, Meena Wood, Martin Norfield, Phillipa Langton and Pip Kings, and my colleagues Judith Gawn, Jan Eldred, Chris Taylor, Jan Novitzky, Anita Hallam and Marie Kerwin. Yanina Dutton's research support and Guistine Kettle's administrative assistance were invaluable. Finally, a warm thank you to Peter Lavender for his insightful suggestions, patience, support and encouragement throughout the writing of this book.

# Preface

While reading this excellent and informative book I became dimly aware of a radio bulletin giving me yet another story connecting religion to identity. It reminded me of Amartya Sen's comment,

> *People's priorities and actions are influenced by all of their affiliations and associations, not merely by religion. For example, the separation of Bangladesh from Pakistan... was based on reasons of language and literature, along with political priorities, not on religion, which both wings of undivided Pakistan shared. To ignore everything other than faith is to obliterate the realities of concerns that have moved people to assert their identities that go well beyond religion.*[1]

Sen argues that to make sense of identity involves making choices. We don't only 'discover' our identity but choose it, making sense of it as we can, making *room for the different loyalties*[2] as Sen puts it. There are conflicting tugs, *disparate pulls*, and sometimes of course we feel there is little choice; that we have been given a set of elements from birth. In Derek Walcott's 'A Far Cry from Africa', the poet illustrates Sen's point: the tug for Walcott lies between his love of the English language and his rage about British rule in his historical African background:

> *Where shall I turn, divided to the vein?*
> *I who have cursed*
> *The drunken officer of British rule, how choose*
> *Between this Africa and the English tongue I love?*
> *Betray them both, or give back what they give?*

1 Amartyan Sen, (2006) *Identity and Violence: the Illusion of Destiny* Penguin, London p 163
2 p 37

*How can I face such slaughter and be cool?*
*How can I turn from Africa and live?*[3]

Walcott's use and love of the English language is an important part of his identity. And it is in the learning of English that people acquire another aspect of their identity and this has been noted by many writers. By and large adults and young people who come to live in Britain choose to learn English for a variety of reasons. All of them are changed by the process and for all of them the language is likely to be a significant part of their identity and their confidence as citizens. This publication aims to look at what the literature tells us about the context in which learners find themselves. It is probably the most thorough recent overview in print about English for speakers of other languages (ESOL) in England.

The literature cited in this book was used to provide evidence in support of the Committee of Inquiry set up by the National Institute of Adult Continuing Education in 2005. The report, *More than a language*,[4] included 39 recommendations on ESOL, most of which have begun to be implemented. Some of the most important were that there should be across-government co-ordination; a minister responsible, and a forum set up to advise the government on some of the directions and trickier issues. All these are in place and the Forum provides an excellent and creative way of ensuring that ESOL is kept at the centre of both the economic and social cohesion agendas. The author, Dr Jane Ward, is both a development officer in NIACE and adviser to the Forum. Previously she was adviser to the Committee of Inquiry, chaired by Derek Grover CB.

The intention is that the work here is used by teacher trainers, researchers, practitioners and policy makers to continue some of the work of the Inquiry: to inform, guide practice, and provide starting points for renewing the thinking on ESOL. Jane Ward argues that ESOL for adults in the UK is a relatively 'under- researched area'. This is a startling observation given that in England more is spent on ESOL for adults than is spent on literacy and numeracy together, an

---

3 p 37.
4 *More than a language: NIACE Committee of Inquiry on English for Speakers of Other Languages (ESOL) Chaired by Derek Grover CB* (NIACE, 2006).

estimated £323 million for 2007-08.[5] The national strategy on literacy, language and numeracy for adults, 'Skills for Life', cost the UK taxpayer £1.7 billion between 2004 and 2007: the highest investment in basic skills for adults in any European country.

*ESOL: The context for the UK today* sets out to explore the seven broad areas covered by the Inquiry. In the chapter on 'policy context' there is a thoughtful exploration of central policy streams, including employment and the role of ESOL in economic recovery, and ESOL in relation to social inclusion – often seen as the two opposing purposes for the 'learning and skills sector'. Helpfully, the author notes that social justice and employment are not incompatible but inter-connected. Chapter 3 examines what we know about ESOL learners and reminds readers that groups are not homogenous. Jane Ward's argument is that provision needs to be more carefully differentiated if it is to meet differing needs and requirements. This is a real curriculum and teaching challenge. In 'What is ESOL?' the author offers what is rarely examined, a close look at what counts as ESOL learning. This is a crucial question for policy makers and funders to get right. The chapter touches on ESOL/EFL, 'embedded' ESOL and ESOL's relationship with literacy work. I was struck by how ESOL is defined by its different purposes as much as its administration, and that the language learning cannot be separated from the economic and social context in which the learning is placed. Formation of identity and the learning content are closely interconnected.

It is this aspect which is explored in Chapter 5, perhaps the most important one for practitioners, on 'Teaching, Learning and Support'. Curiously, it was in relation to teacher training and development (Chapter 6) that the Committee of Inquiry had the hardest challenge – to understand its complexity, make a judgement about its efficacy and speed, and encourage a balance between high quality and utility. It was also the area on which we had the most recommendations not adopted by the government! The Committee's view was that although there was rapid change taking place, encouragement was needed to enhance the development of new programmes and greater

---

5 Letter from Mark Haysom, 24 January 2007 (*Hansard*): Cost of ESOL since 2000: 2000-01 £103m; 2001-02 £185m; 2002-03 £235m; 2003-04 £267m; 2004-05 £279m; 2005-06 More than £270m (est); 2006-07 £306m (est); 2007-08 £323m (est).

numbers of teachers. If teacher training were more robustly addressed, went our argument, quality might improve and demand might better be met. Jane Ward concludes that quality of provision and the teacher training improvement are inextricably linked.

In Chapter 7, 'Funding', the author has been challenged by the fact that each month that goes by would require its re-writing. Useful, however, is the framework, and the broad thinking. Shifts of policy, like sand, have meant that at the time of writing there are six completely separate national surveys aimed at finding out what is going on in the ESOL provision, each one put out by a government or national agency. This in itself must be a record. What it tells us is that there are major concerns and that current approaches are 'not inevitable'. In Jane Ward's concluding Chapter 8 the themes are drawn together, with a thoughtful request for fresh thinking on the purposes of ESOL in today's society to both empower learners and provide the necessary skills the nation needs. *The shifts in learner populations and demand require radical solutions,* Jane Ward suggests, *Reformist tinkering round the edges of ESOL is unlikely to result in the fundamental changes needed…*The argument is well put: if we want a more just and equitable society then we need to link language learning more skilfully to the social contexts of exclusion and disadvantage. I would only add that identity and the learning of English is fundamental to this thinking.

In Marion Molteno's fine book *A Language in Common*[6] she describes this connection between identity and learning English through a set of short stories based on the author's years as an adult education tutor in London, mainly among women from India and Pakistan. The society in which they find themselves is alien, often hostile. Yet as they discover more about each other friendships develop across the boundaries of language and culture. In the first story, 'The uses of literacy' she describes the setting up of an ESOL group for women only but unfortunately the posters are not quite clear enough and when Mr H. S. Ramgarhia arrives she feels obliged to teach him individually, intending at the end of the lesson to ask him to move to another centre where there was a mixed class:

6 Molteno, Marion (1987) *A Language in Common* The Women's Press, London (now republished by Longstone Books, London).

*...I would explain the situation to him gently, and direct him to the mixed class two miles down the road. But at the end of the morning it was Mr H. S. Ramgarhia who made the speech, not me. He stood up, and put his hands behind his back in a way that made it clear what was going to happen. I stood up too, to receive it: 'I have to thank you for this most illuminating lesson', he said, his craggy head inclined towards me with great simplicity. 'I have wished all my life to be an educated man, but until now the need to provide for my family has made it impossible. I left school very young. God has blessed my work, and enabled me to provide for my sons the education I could not have. Now my sons can support me, and I have the leisure to learn. All the English I know I have learnt without tuition. I listened to Englishmen speak in the days when the British were still in India. Now I am in the UK, I listen to the radio and television. But reading and writing have remained a difficulty for me. I spend time every day in the library, trying to read the newspapers, but many words escape my understanding. Now I have a teacher, I am sure I can begin to attain my life's ambition. I wish to thank you for providing me with this opportunity.'*

What Molteno captures in her book is the way in which adult students perceive the value of English language, and that learning this language, as Jane Ward makes clear, does not happen in isolation but in a social context that matters to us all.

*Peter Lavender*

*'By words the mind is winged'*
Aristophanes

This book is for all the students whose lives have been in
some way enriched and liberated through learning English.

# 1 Introduction

The field of English for Speakers of Other Languages (ESOL)[1] is one of the huge challenges facing the post-16 learning and skills sector in the UK. English language is important because it liberates people to take control over their lives, achieve greater prosperity and participate in social and civic society. Significant changes in migration trends have led to new and increased demands for English language learning. At the same time long-term settled immigrants continue to need access to English classes. Migrants bring a wealth of skills, knowledge and talent and make a substantial and positive contribution to the economic, social and cultural life of the nation (Refugee Council, 2002). In return, it is vital that they are supported to acquire the English language they need to live and thrive in the UK.

Migration has long been a feature of the UK demography (Phillimore *et al.*, 2006; Winder, 2005). Far from being static, it is a dynamic process in which there are both continuities and shifts. The migrant profile alters in response to both internal and external catalysts such as war, genocide, home and international policy changes, poverty, and increasing globalisation that has led to more flexible movement of populations, labour and capital across the world (Berkeley *et al.*, 2006; Zetter *et al.*, 2006). This makes migration difficult to describe, as data are only ever accurate for a brief period, if ever. It is even harder to predict migration patterns with certainty. We do know, however, that the last 15 years have been marked by rising numbers of refugees and people seeking asylum in the UK, and although numbers have started to fall, the trend could reverse again

1 The term ESOL is used to cover all English language tuition for adult speakers of other languages. This includes all settings where teaching and learning takes place, and encompasses embedded language support to enable learners to access other subjects as well as discrete English language provision.

1

in response to global events. Migration for reunion with families and spouses continues, and patterns of economic migration have altered in response to labour market changes, especially a huge increase in migrant workers following the expansion of the European Union in 2004 (Berkeley *et al.*, 2006; Zetter *et al.*, 2006).

This has had a major impact on individuals, communities and employers as populations and workforces have become more diverse and complex. Inevitably this has affected English language learning demands, requiring all concerned to take a fresh look at policy, strategy, funding and practice. English language learners have always included settled immigrants, short-term migrants, refugees, asylum seekers, and overseas students and their spouses. However, in recent years the balance has altered, numbers have risen, and learners' countries of origin have become more diverse. Furthermore, current approaches to providing and funding ESOL make it difficult to respond adequately to wide-ranging and multiple needs and priorities. At the same time the inspectorates have deep concerns about the quality of much ESOL provision, many areas struggle to recruit sufficient qualified teachers, and funding bodies are struggling to meet the costs of rising demand from finite resources. For the National Institute of Adult Continuing Education (NIACE) the enormous problems besetting ESOL amounted to a crisis that needed urgent attention. Thus an independent Committee of Inquiry was established in November 2005 to investigate ESOL in England.

The content of this book is drawn from the findings of the investigation that was conducted for the Inquiry, which reported in October 2006. It provides an in-depth discussion of the matters raised in the Committee report, *More than a Language* (NIACE, 2006), drawing on articles, research studies and policy documents to identify and illuminate the major contemporary concerns and challenges for English language learning and learners. It provides a snapshot of ESOL at a particular time. This is a time in which the context in which ESOL is operating is constantly changing so that shifts in policy and funding subsequent to the completion of this book are inevitable.

The primary reference point is England since the UK government's *Skills for Life* policy, which was the focus of the NIACE Inquiry, relates solely to England. Many of the questions discussed will be relevant for Scotland, Wales and Northern Ireland, countries which are also experiencing increased migration with consequent population shifts and demand for English language development, although they might play out in diverse ways in the different national contexts.

The year 1990 has been taken as the starting point, as this includes literature from the decade leading up to the period of massive and rapid change in literacy, language and numeracy provision in England triggered by the publication of the report of the Moser Committee (DfEE, 1999). The ESOL working group report, *Breaking the Language Barriers* (DfEE, 2000), highlighted the salient features of ESOL and made a series of recommendations that ensured the inclusion of ESOL in the *Skills for Life* policy. These developments, with the demographic changes outlined above, can be viewed as altering the nature of the field of ESOL in substantial and significant ways.

Many of the matters raised in *Breaking the Language Barriers* remain live, albeit with different emphases. As populations of ESOL learners and policy landscapes have shifted, additional and urgent questions and areas of concern have emerged. These changes have raised fundamental questions. What is ESOL and what is it for? Who are the learners, what do they want to learn and how? Where does ESOL best sit in strategy and organisational structures? What does excellent and effective provision look like and how can we ensure this is offered to all? Has sufficient attention between paid to gender dimensions? What kind of workforce do we want and how can we recruit and train these staff? Do we need more research to inform developments in provision and practice?

Vast increases in demand have also led to questions about financing ESOL; is the current offer of free ESOL funded by the state either sustainable or equitable? Should the state provide more funding and if so, how much? Should some individuals or their employers be asked to pay towards the costs of their tuition and, if so, on what basis? How can more effective collaborative working across government departments and inter-agency provision be put in place to provide more holistic and effective approaches to satisfy need? These concerns have provoked intense debates among and between policy and funding agencies, researchers, and practitioners who have as yet agreed few definitive solutions.

Sources to inform an exploration of these questions include policy documents, inspection reports and guidance documents that help to provide background and contextual information. The book does not seek to replicate Barton and Pitt's (2003) literature review which provides an outline of the themes, content, stance and evidence base of the ESOL literature. It aims to construct a comprehensive picture of contemporary thinking and concerns through documents that have been selected to illustrate and illuminate current contexts, challenges and debates. Inevitably, some of the recent studies shine a light on long-standing questions or confirm findings that are already well known to experienced practitioners. Others offer new perspectives or relate established knowledge to the contemporary context. Recent studies, especially those carried out by the National Research and Development Centre (NRDC) for adult literacy and numeracy have added to the ESOL research base. Despite this, ESOL for adults in the UK is a relatively under-researched area, and there are omissions and underdeveloped areas in theory and research (Barton and Pitt, 2003; Brooks *et al.*, 2001; Ivanič and Tseng, 2005; Pitt, 2005). These will be identified in the text which is organised in the following chapters:

2.  Policy context
3.  Who are the learners?
4.  What is ESOL?
5.  Teaching, learning and support
6.  Teacher recruitment and training
7.  Funding
8.  Conclusion

# 2 Policy context

The relevance of policy and strategies relating to English language teaching and learning is obvious. However, to look at them in isolation would provide a partial and simplistic picture as many other policy areas touch English language learners, not least those relating to immigration, race and integration (Hamilton and Hillier, 2006). This chapter will explore ESOL in the policy contexts of *Skills for Life*, employment and skills and social justice.

## Skills for Life

The origins of the most recent drive to improve language skills can be located in the post-16 learning policies of the New Labour government that came to power in 1997. This government promoted the creation of a learning society as one of the primary mechanisms for achieving its twin aims of increasing economic prosperity and social and civic regeneration. To bring this about, it introduced policies to expand and promote learning opportunities to all sectors of the population, especially those least likely to access them:

> As well as securing our economic future, learning has a wider contribution. It helps to make ours a civilised society, develops the spiritual side of our lives and promotes active citizenship. Learning enables people to play a full part in their community. It strengthens the family, the neighbourhood and consequently the nation. (DfEE, 1998, p. 7)

This broad vision was accompanied by an increasing realisation that limited literacy, language and numeracy skills could inhibit people's capacity to benefit from measures to advance both economic prosperity and social justice. Concerns about the health of the nation's literacy and numeracy skills prompted the government to establish a committee, chaired by Claus Moser, to consider adult basic skills (the term for literacy, numeracy and ESOL commonly used at the time) and make recommendations for effective post-school basic skills provision. In what came to be known as the Moser Report, this committee drew on the findings of the International Adult Literacy Survey to conclude that approximately seven million adults in England and Wales, that is about one in five adults, had poor literacy and numeracy skills (DfEE, 1999).

The Moser report spelled out the consequences of this, drawing on published research including ALBSU's investigation of the intergenerational effects of poor basic skills (1993a) and the cost to industry (1993b), and Bynner and Parsons longitudinal study (1997) that identified a correlation between poor basic skills and social and economic disadvantage. The committee recommended improving poor basic skills as an effective strategy for addressing these disadvantages for the benefit of individuals, their families, communities and the economy (DfEE, 1999). While the figures cited are necessarily estimates, and some of the evidence is controversial (Hamilton and Barton, 2000; Papen, 2005; Robinson, 1997) they did serve to shock the government into action. The field received an unprecedented amount of government attention and funding in the wake of this report, resulting in new strategies and a plethora of initiatives and interventions. Implementation groups were established to develop a national strategy, *Skills for Life*, for improving adult basic skills in England (DfEE, 2001a). Since the Moser Committee had not addressed ESOL in any depth, one of these groups was tasked with considering the implications of the report for English for Speakers of Other Languages.

This marked a significant change as policy relating to ESOL had, up to this point, been neither coherent nor integrated with adult literacy (Hamilton and Hillier, 2006; Hamilton and Merrifield, 2000; and Rosenberg, 2006). ESOL was included in the remit of the Adult Literacy and Basic Skills Unit (ALBSU) from 1984. Despite this, commentators such as Hamilton and Hillier (2006) and Rosenberg (2006) suggest it never received sufficient recognition and attention as a separate curriculum area, and ALBSU itself acknowledged limitations in its ESOL work in an article in the Spring 1992 Newsletter. This was attributed to factors that include a political climate hostile to immigrants. Some ESOL practitioners were also resistant to association with literacy and numeracy, emphasising the differences in the nature of the student cohorts, their education backgrounds and learning needs as well as ESOL pedagogy. At policy level there appeared to be inadequate recognition of the distinctive nature of ESOL students, language learning needs and pedagogical practices. Lack of funding was also a factor and the government rejected funding for an ALBSU proposal to develop ESOL to meet the need identified in its 1989 survey (ALBSU, 1989). Literacy and ESOL classes were often funded from different sources, with Section 11 of the Local Government Act 1966 a principal source of funding for adult ESOL provision. This changed in 1992 when the Further and Higher Education Act introduced a new funding regime. Literacy, numeracy and ESOL all became eligible for the same funding stream through the new funding body, the Further Education Funding Council.

*Breaking the Language Barriers*, the report of the ESOL implementation group, identified the distinct features of ESOL and made a series of recommendations, the first of which was:

> All developments in the national adult basic skills strategy must address ESOL needs alongside but distinct from basic literacy and numeracy and this should be a specific responsibility of the Adult Basic Skills Strategy Unit. (DfEE, 2000, p. 21)

Further recommendations concerned establishing baseline data, participation and achievement targets, funding, meeting need, materials, quality standards, curriculum, qualifications, teacher training and quality. Language was subsequently included in the *Skills for Life* policy. However, the extent to which either the distinctive nature of ESOL or these recommendations have been taken into account in the implementation of the *Skills for Life* policy is questionable.

Priority groups identified in the *Skills for Life* strategy included 'refugees and asylum seekers, and others who do not speak English as a first language' (DfEE, 2001a). A high profile Adult Basic Skills Strategy Unit[2] was created in the then Department for Education and Employment, to lead and oversee the development of a national

---

2 This subsequently became the *Skills for Life* Strategy Unit

infrastructure. This aimed to develop a strong, centralised infrastructure and standards to bring about improvements in quality and equality. The Unit introduced standardised core curricula for literacy, numeracy and ESOL; teaching and assessment materials; qualifications for learners; and teacher training standards. ESOL Pathfinders were set up in 2002 to develop and test this infrastructure, using a framework that mirrored that introduced for adult literacy and numeracy. The outcomes and findings of these Pathfinders were evaluated using qualitative and quantitative methods, and the findings reported in two documents by Dalziel and Sofres (2005a and 2005b). The ESOL field has undoubtedly reaped many positive benefits. The profile has been enhanced, funding has increased to unprecedented levels, and many more learners have had the opportunity to access provision (DfES, 2003b).

The NIACE ESOL inquiry (NIACE, 2006) and researchers such as Baynham *et al.* (2007), Papen (2005), and Pitt (2005) have found that opinions of the new structures vary. Benefits identified by teachers include more coherence and consistency, improvements in quality, and support for teachers to develop. Other voices are more critical. They consider that centralisation has brought financial advantages at the cost of producing an inflexible view of what is right; one that imposes limitations on teachers' and learners' autonomy. Furthermore, writers such as Hamilton (2006b) suggest, centralisation has brought in an audit culture that generates targets and quality improvement criteria which result in practice that neither delivers the targets nor fully coincides with learners' main concerns. This is particularly so when the latter do not coincide with government priorities. The space for alternative discourses has also been constricted, although some writers illustrate how practitioners have managed to use their agency to find creative ways of sidestepping constraints to respond to learners' diverse needs and purposes (Barton and Papen, 2005; Hamilton and Hillier, 2006; Roberts *et al.*, 2004).

A recurring question is whether the distinctive features of ESOL have been preserved within the *Skills for Life* initiatives. Has the literacy model diverted attention from the fundamental language learning dimension of ESOL with its different and diverse learner profiles and pedagogic practices? Early strategy documents in England referred primarily to literacy and numeracy (DfEE, 1999 and

2001a). The updated *Skills for Life* strategy (DfES, 2003b) makes more overt references to language. Even so, the document contains scant recognition of the particular ESOL aspects of its four key themes: boosting demand, increasing capacity, raising standards and learner achievement. Yet these areas are the sites of the major challenges the ESOL field currently faces: responding to high levels of learner demand, insufficient trained teachers, and fierce debates concerning pedagogical approaches, what constitutes high quality teaching and learning and what are the most appropriate measures of English language learners' achievements. Similarly, other policy documents and research studies into different aspects of literacy, language and numeracy do not disaggregate the English language aspects, failing to explore and make explicit the commonalities and differences, and the influences of variables such as language and ethnicity which are important to further our knowledge and develop practice.

What does it mean for ESOL provision and pedagogic practice if developments owe more to an overarching adult literacy model than to second language acquisition theory? There is little evidence of any significant research or examination of whether, or how far and in what ways, literacy models are appropriate for language teaching and learning or not. These models themselves have been the subject of debate and critique by writers such as Crowther *et al.* (2001), Hamilton and Merrifield (2000) and Papen (2005). A further concern is whether adoption of the literacy framework has obscured the opportunity offered by the introduction of the *Skills for Life* strategy to undertake a root and branch re-examination of ESOL. Questions concern the extent to which models of provision and pedagogy developed from the early 1970s to respond to the needs of immigrants primarily from the Indian subcontinent have been modified to respond to contemporary circumstances. Arguably, a radical critique could have gone a long way to avoid or resolve many of the challenges burdening ESOL that will be outlined in subsequent chapters.

## Employment and skills

Government policies relating to the broader learning and skills policy terrain in which *Skills for Life* is located have consistently affirmed the importance of learning in combating social injustice as well as improving productivity (DfES, 2003c and DfES, 2005f). A major government priority is to increase economic growth and enhance prosperity by enhancing the skills of the workforce. This is accompanied by recognition that enhancing skills promotes social mobility, helps to tackle matters such as poverty, poor health and crime, and increases community cohesion and democratic and cultural participation. There is, however, a tension in current policy between learning for employment purposes and learning for social inclusion, and writers such as Papen (2005) suggest that there has been an increasing privileging of the economic imperative. Consequently, skills have become the dominant discourse, outweighing that relating to the wider purposes that learners identify for their learning.

There can be little doubt that developing English language and employment skills are of vital importance to migrants. There is compelling evidence that securing and progressing in employment is one of the most important factors in successful settlement. It provides economic independence, enhances self-esteem, and offers opportunities to speak and learn English through interaction with other workers (DWP, 2005; Dustmann and Fabbri, 2003; Home Office, 2005a and 2005b; ODPM, 2004a; Phillimore *et al.*, 2006). In view of this, the evidence indicating the high levels of exclusion from the labour market or underemployment of adult speakers of other languages is particularly disturbing. A recent investigation of ethnic penalties in the labour market carried out for the Department of Work and Pensions concludes that:

> ...at the beginning of the twenty-first century, a number of ethnic minority groups, notably Pakistani, Bangladeshi, Black Caribbean and Black African men continue to experience higher unemployment rates, greater concentrations in routine and semi-routine work and lower hourly earnings than do members of the comparison group of British and other whites. (Heath and Cheung, 2006, p. 18)

First generation migrants, those who were born abroad and migrated to the UK, tend to experience more ethnic penalties than the subsequent generations born in the UK, and language is one of the multiple factors that limit their access to the labour market (Heath and Cheung, 2006). Evidence indicates that shortages of appropriate opportunities to work mean that bilingual adults are often concentrated in low-paid, unskilled roles with few promotion prospects. Thus they are caught in the poverty trap despite often possessing the skills and personal qualities for advancement in the labour market. Moreover, many migrants with skilled and professional employment histories encounter massive barriers to accessing employment commensurate with their skills and abilities (Aldridge *et al.*, 2005; Bloch, 2002 and 2004; Hurstfield *et al.*, 2004; Waddington, 2005).

Employment profiles differ between and within groups, with members of some communities particularly vulnerable to unemployment or underemployment. Tackey *et al.* (2006), in a study of barriers to employment for Pakistani and Bangladeshi adults in Britain carried out for the Department of Work and Pensions, found that Pakistani and Bangladeshi adults are severely disadvantaged in the labour market compared to white and other major minority groups. Polish migrant workers have high rates of employment while fewer than half the working-age adults of Pakistani and Bangladeshi origin, and only 12.2 per cent of people from Somalia are in work (Heath and Cheung, 2006; Home Office, 2005a; Kyambi, 2005). Gender is a significant factor in underemployment as women's participation rates are consistently lower than those of men, and their skills and employment potential often overlooked (Kofman *et al.*, 2005). This is an under-researched area, but we do know that this trend is particularly marked amongst Pakistani and Bangladeshi women where the level of labour market participation is disproportionately low (Tackey *et al.*, 2006).

Education background and English language skills have a considerable impact on employment prospects. Immigrants with fluent English language are 20 per cent more likely to be in employment and earn approximately 20 per cent more than those with underdeveloped language skills (Bloch 2002, Dustmann and Fabbri, 2003). The severe labour market disadvantage of Pakistani and Bangladeshi adults can in part be attributed to low levels of proficiency in English; only 4 per cent of Bangladeshi and 28 per cent of Pakistani women aged 45–64 speak fluent English (Tackey *et al.*, 2006). Many refugees also face considerable barriers in entering the employment market at levels commensurate with their skills and experience (Bloch, 2002; Bloch, 2004; Hurstfield *et al.*, 2004).

Settled immigrants, migrant workers and refugees can make a

powerful contribution to addressing the skills shortages at all levels of the UK labour market that reports such as Leitch (2005 and 2006) predict will increase over the next 10 years, although, curiously, Leitch has little to say about migration and migrant workers. The disadvantages of a low-skilled workforce are forecast to become more acute as globalisation, coupled with demographic and technological changes, results in an increasingly competitive global marketplace requiring a more highly-skilled economy. Thus, the national strategy to improve skills and productivity (DfES, 2003c), updated in a 2005 White Paper (DfES, 2005f) is founded on a drive to improve national productivity through improving skills. It focuses on learning to upgrade the vocational and basic skills of low-skilled workers and adults not currently in work. Strategies and initiatives focused on supporting unemployed adults to re-enter the labour market are also founded on a belief that supporting them to develop literacy, language and numeracy skills is a fundamental element of these processes (DWP, 2006).

The White Paper also reaffirms the government's commitment to improving literacy, language and numeracy skills, and emphasises the level 2 functional skills that are viewed as necessary for productive working. A major limitation of this policy as far as ESOL is concerned is that it does not take into account the language development needed to equip professionals and skilled bilingual workers to operate above the level 2 threshold, even though a need for a high-skilled workforce is identified by Leitch (2005 and 2006). Highly qualified and skilled adult speakers of other languages can be further disadvantaged by policies to reduce national levels of 'worklessness' (DWP, 2006). The imperative to move people into jobs can force these adults to abandon their English language studies and force them to take up low-skilled, low-waged employment that is well below their potential. This does little to bring about greater economic advancement or social justice.

## Social justice

The drive to combat social exclusion requires other matters, including raising education achievement and aspirations, community capacity building, democratic participation, health, and social cohesion, to be addressed at the same time as economic factors. The causes and consequences of social exclusion tend to be inextricably linked and mutually reinforcing (ODPM, 2004a), and some are rooted in deeply entrenched societal inequalities. Consequently language proficiency is rarely the sole cause, but is often a contributory factor. For the same reason, developing language is unlikely to offer a sole solution. However, it can make a powerful contribution, especially when founded on participatory approaches such as the Reflect approach described by Archer (2005) and offered as an element of multiple and coherent actions for change.

Without language skills people are more likely to continue living in circumstances of poverty. In contrast, enhanced language proficiency not only improves employment prospects, but enables adults to act with knowledge and confidence to access and shape the existing institutions and structures of society. Moreover, the benefits of learning tend to ripple far beyond their immediate context as shown in the study to identify the wider benefits of learning conducted by Schuller *et al.* (2004). Taking part in learning to develop language can also build the self-esteem and confidence, that alongside cultural and societal knowledge, support people's well-being and ability to settle and live independent, healthy, fulfilling lives.

*Skills for Life* has from its beginning sought to address both the economic and social inclusion agendas (DfEE, 2001a). While many migrants are employed in well-paid occupations, others live in disadvantaged areas where the communication and access difficulties associated with lower-level language skills can compound the challenges they face:

> Social exclusion has complex and multidimensional causes and consequences, creating deep and long-lasting problems for individual families, for the economy and for society as a whole. It can pass from generation to generation: children's life chances are strongly affected by their parents' circumstances, such as their income and the place they live. (SEU, 2004, p. 1)

Accordingly, *Skills for Life* and Skills policies are not the only policy areas relevant to ESOL. The government's vision of a strong and fair society is very relevant to adult speakers of other languages. Language is a major factor in enabling bilingual adults to understand, access and contribute to shaping the services and opportunities associated with implementation of policies across many areas of policy and legislation, particularly those relating to social inclusion, children and families, immigration, settlement, citizenship, sports and culture, neighbourhood renewal, and combating racism and community cohesion (Commission on Integration and Cohesion, 2006 and 2007; DCLG, 2006; HM Government, 2004 and 2006; Home Office, 2003, 2005a and 2005b; Lyons, 2006; ODPM, 2003, 2004a and 2004b; SEU, 2004).

Communication, for instance, has been identified as an elemental factor in building cohesive communities (Home Office, 2005a and 2005b). This applies to all communities, and Zetter *et al.* (2006), in their exploration of immigration, social cohesion and social capital, spell out some of the complexities and contradictions inherent in the concept of community cohesion, with the consequent challenges for policy development and implementation. They suggest that there tends to be more focus on the need for immigrants to learn English than on the contribution established populations can make to foster harmonious communities:

> In short, while immigrant communities remain in the spotlight, it is neither evident what it is they might be cohering to, nor clear who is, or should be, doing the cohering. (Zetter *et al.*, 2006, p. 8)

Whatever the resolution of these challenges, English language will be essential if people are to take an active part in the dialogues and processes introduced to facilitate greater social cohesion.

In considering the role of local government, the Department of Local Government and Communities and the Lyons inquiry have stressed the importance of engagement with, as well as accountability to, citizens and promoted their involvement in procuring and delivering local services (DCLG 2006, Lyons 2006 and 2007). Regeneration and developing sustainable communities relies on strong leadership, effective delivery and the involvement of local communities (ODPM 2003, 2004b and 2005). English language proficiency can enable speakers of other languages to contribute to consultation and planning processes as well as take on effective leadership roles and gain employment.

Language development can work alongside other political, economic and social solutions to social exclusion. These are more likely to be realised through more effective co-ordination of policy and statutory and voluntary services. However, wider policies rarely address the potential impact of language on implementation and the implications of this for ESOL provision. There is little evidence of meaningful liaison between different national government departments, or agencies at regional level, to ensure that there is sufficient tuition available with relevant content. This is not just a curriculum matter. Neither policy development nor planning and funding streams for ESOL learning and programme delivery are consistently aligned with those of other agencies and organisations. Consequently, there is a lack of creative cross-departmental co-operation to develop a strategic vision that works across different departments and agencies at national, regional and local levels.

There is, for instance, recognition across government that employment is a critical factor in settlement and reducing inequalities, and that bringing this about will be dependent on inter-agency working using approaches that draw on specialist expertise from a range of agencies and sectors (DWP, 2005; Home Office, 2005b). Yet at ground level the activities of agencies and organisations frequently remain unconnected to learning programmes in the ways that are most likely to bring this about. There are as yet few models or funding streams aligned to support collaborative working, and ESOL responses are still in development. This limits their benefit to learners who do not experience coherent, mutually reinforcing, services. Potential exists for developing a more cohesive response to ESOL learners' priorities through cross-departmental planning, funding, service delivery and multi-agency working that has not as yet been adequately explored.

As ESOL learners are not a homogeneous group, their aspirations and learning needs are multiple and diverse. Addressing them will require a range of focused responses. The next chapter will outline features of learners' backgrounds that should inform this planning.

# 3   Who are the learners?

Knowing who the learners are and what they want to learn is critical to any discussion of ESOL. This chapter will illuminate the backgrounds, aspirations and priorities of learners through consideration of the circumstances of adults from settled communities, refugees and asylum seekers, migrant workers and adults living in rural areas. ESOL learners are extremely heterogeneous (Dalziel and Sofres, 2005b; Ivanič *et al.*, 2006; Roberts *et al.*, 2004), and it is recognised that the groups discussed are neither static nor internally homogeneous. Nevertheless, identifying common background features does serve to illuminate traits and features of learner demand, the complexity and the challenges entailed in formulating adequate responses.

Predicting levels of demand for services, including English language learning is difficult because patterns of immigration and employment of migrant labour constantly fluctuate. There is little readily available information, and a paucity of accurate quantitative data relating to immigration, language levels, learning needs and achievements. The Office of National Statistics (ONS, 2007) recognises that international migration and internal movement of immigrants is one the most difficult components of population change and is prioritising work to improve migration and population statistics.

Robinson and Reeve (2006), in their study of the consequences and experiences of immigration at neighbourhood level, note the lack of evidence of the numbers, socio-economic and demographic profiles, skills levels, qualifications and settlement patterns of new migrants. This constrains the ability of national, regional and local bodies and providers to formulate strategic responses to demand for ESOL. We do know, however, that the number of learners accessing ESOL provision has been steadily increasing over the last two decades, and their backgrounds have become more diverse. Some areas are experiencing unprecedented demand for English language tuition, but this is unevenly spread across the country. Forty-two per cent of migrants are living in London, attracted by its role as a global city and the prospects of work, whereas only three per cent are in the North East where there are less obvious employment prospects (Kyambi, 2005).

A survey of language need carried out for the Basic Skills Agency in 1996 (Carr-Hill *et al.*) estimated that 450,000 people needed support to develop English language, but that only half of them were either learning English or had attended English classes in the past. It is difficult to determine precise figures relating to prospective learners unable to access English language provision because language need is not systematically recorded in data relating to migration. However, anecdotal evidence gathered by the NIACE Inquiry into ESOL indicates that the huge unmet demand identified by Carr-Hill *et al.* (1996) and in London by Rees and Sunderland (1990 and 1991) has swollen, and is now replicated in many areas of the county (NIACE, 2006). The situation is especially acute in cities, towns and rural areas to which asylum seekers have been dispersed, or where large numbers of migrant workers have entered employment.

ESOL learners come from diverse backgrounds. These were broadly categorised in *Breaking the Language Barriers* (DfEE, 2000) as settled communities, refugees and asylum seekers, migrant workers and partners and spouses of learners. As this report also noted, the needs of learners within these groups vary considerably depending on a number of factors that include 'their aspirations, educational background, language and literacy background and aptitude for learning languages' (DfEE, 2000, p. 4). Since *Breaking the Language Barriers* was published, demographic shifts have altered the profile of learner demand and we have gained more insights into the complexities of defining identity, status and learning interests (Aldridge and Waddington, 2002; Aldridge and Tuckett, 2003; Armstrong and Heathcote, 2003; Atkin *et al.*, 2005; DfES, 2006c). Attributing membership of a category is problematic since a person's identity does not always fit with legal definitions of their status. When does a refugee stop being a refugee for instance? Furthermore, membership can be fluid since individuals flow between categories as their legal status or life plans change; for example when asylum seekers are granted refugee status or European migrant workers decide to settle in the UK.

Research has consistently shown that most recently arrived adult speakers of other languages, have a fierce desire to learn English (Bloch, 2002 and 2004; Waddington, 2005; Yai *et al*., 2005). Priorities might be common to members of one or more groups and a range of factors influence the type of provision they want to take up as well as their ability to access it. Their main concerns can be determined by socio-economic, demographic, geographic or cultural influences that can cut across the different groups. Living in a rural area, having a disability or learning difficulty, or factors such as class, gender, age and employment aspirations can be a more significant determinant of learning priorities and interests than a category constructed on the basis of immigration status. What is certain is that, with few exceptions, learners attending ESOL classes will be extremely heterogeneous with diverse educational histories, aspirations and learning needs.

## Settled communities

Learners in settled communities include long-settled migrants as well as more recent arrivals and refugees, but robust data are not available to indicate the proportions of each. The purposes and aspirations of different groups such as established residents, new arrivals, people of Caribbean heritage, and second-generation young people often differ considerably.

Many settled residents decide to develop more fluency in English many years after arrival (Baynham *et al*., 2007; Dalziel and Sofres, 2005b). A frequent catalyst for language learning is insecure employment or unemployment. Tackey *et al*. (2006) observed that traditional manufacturing industries employed high numbers of immigrants, especially, but not exclusively, Pakistani and Bangladeshi men who comprise a high proportion of settled residents. They found that the decline of these industries has, therefore, produced disproportionately high rates of unemployment amongst middle-aged men from these groups. Moreover, Pakistani and Bangladeshi adults have the lowest levels of English of all the major minority ethnic groups and this can inhibit their prospects of securing alternative employment.

Gender is significant. Some women have been in England for many years but never learned English, exemplified by the low levels of fluency in English amongst Pakistani and Bangladeshi women cited in the previous chapter (Heath and Cheung, 2006; Tackey *et al.*, 2006). Gender oppression, family opposition, lack of independence or other gender-related cultural factors can restrict opportunities to take up learning. Structural inadequacies such as lack of information about opportunities, or failure to organise accessible provision or childcare might also have prevented women from attending English classes in the past. Many women have been forced to rely on family members for support, but find this support dissipating as families disperse, couples divorce, or death leaves older adults to cope alone.

Drawing in these adults can require a great deal of outreach work, and targeted, community- or home-based provision which is both time consuming and expensive. This means that their needs are sometimes overshadowed by the more overt demands of new arrivals, and their opportunities constrained because classes are filled without them (Dalziel and Sofres, 2005b). Some, but not all, providers see little incentive to invest in outreach work to attract learners such as older Somali women or young Bangladeshi mothers when they already have bulging classes and long waiting lists. When this happens swathes of the population are excluded; often women whose lives might be significantly enhanced by the autonomy, opportunities and wider horizons they could gain through enhancing their English language.

Research into gender and migration by Kofman *et al.* (2005) shows that family migration, where spouses, fiancés and fiancées join settled communities, is highly feminised, with significantly more wives and fiancées entering than husbands and fiancés, the majority from states outside the EU. A number of these women are highly proficient in English, but many others need to improve their proficiency in English but are not eligible for free state-funded learning provision for three years, or one year for those eligible under the spouses' residency rule. This rule, described in an article by Sir Bernard Crick (2006) as 'stupid', disbars them from free provision at the time when they need to learn as quickly as possible to support them to settle. It is much harder, for example, for young women to find work or go through their first pregnancy in an unfamiliar health environment without language and cultural knowledge. As their ability to communicate is severely constrained, they can become isolated or, Crick (2006) asserts, remain, 'submerged in their own communities and may already have suffered permanent communication problems with mainstream society'. A recent NRDC research study of effective practice in ESOL has also demonstrated that delays in starting to learn English can have a detrimental effect on the rate at which adults learn and progress (Baynham *et al.*, 2007).

Patois speakers from Caribbean countries often have particular English language learning needs that Dalziel and Sofres (2005b) and Millman (2005) say have not received adequate attention in the *Skills for Life* strategy. They observe that neither ESOL nor literacy provision neatly meets Caribbean language speakers' English language learning needs. These adults do not necessarily identify as speakers of other languages or as ESOL learners and their preferences tend to be for attending literacy classes. However, ESOL and literacy teachers' understanding of Caribbean language issues is often, Millman suggests, underdeveloped which limits their capacity to respond effectively to these learners. There is little designated provision for this group, although there are examples such as City College Birmingham which has recruited and trained Jamaican teachers and is developing 'English for speakers of Caribbean Languages' provision. Some African learners who have English as one of their languages encounter similar barriers (Pitt, 2005).

## Refugees and asylum seekers

As noted earlier, membership of these groups is not fixed. There is more clarity about what the terms mean in terms of legal status. The definitions adopted here, using the definition of a refugee decided at the 1951 United Nations Convention relating to the status of refugees, are as follows:

> A refugee is someone who has fled, or is unable to return to, their country of origin because of a 'well founded fear of persecution due to race, religion, nationality, membership of a social group or political opinion'. In the UK a person becomes a refugee by claiming asylum and having that claim approved.

> An asylum seeker is a person who has claimed refugee status and is waiting for a decision on this claim.

Refugees and asylum seekers arrive in the UK from many different countries seeking refuge from war, persecution, genocide and/or torture. In 2000, the government introduced a policy of dispersing asylum seekers across the UK, often to cities and towns with no experiences of providing services for asylum seekers. As a result they often find themselves in localities with no source of community support trying to access local agencies and service providers who lack the expertise or capacity to provide appropriate responses (Robinson and Reeve, 2006) Similarly, as Hodge *et al.* (2004) in their case study of asylum seekers attending ESOL classes in Blackburn, and Waddington (2005) in the report of her action research on auditing and developing the skills of asylum seekers, have found, ESOL providers in dispersal areas often have no history of working with asylum seekers and refugees. Accordingly, teachers are unfamiliar with the background circumstances that can affect learning and have to learn how to adapt their teaching and learning approaches for their new learner groups. These difficulties are exacerbated by the lack of research-based evidence relating to migration profiles and experiences of living in local communities that could help service providers to formulate effective responses (Robinson and Reeve, 2006).

As studies of the lives of refugees and/or asylum seekers such as Dumper (2002), Hodge *et al.* (2004), and the Refugee Council (2002 and 2005b) remind us, asylum seekers' lives have been fractured. They are often destitute or living in poverty with the associated loss of dignity, self-esteem and sometimes hope. They are forced to subsist on very limited financial resources, and are not permitted to work. This can fuel a loss of self-assurance (Yai *et al.*, 2005). They may be suffering from stress, mental ill health or illness resulting from the traumatic experiences, fear and confusion involved in leaving their country. These are often intensified by the process of seeking asylum, by the uncertainties of waiting for a decision on their application, by denial of the right to work and, for some, hostility from established communities.

Asylum seekers frequently encounter welcome and friendship, but too often tensions and divisions arise between different communities. Robinson and Reeve (2006) observe that this is more likely to occur in communities where access to employment is limited, scarce resources such as health and housing are perceived to be unfairly distributed, and the established populations have had little previous contact with migrants. Zetter *et al.* (2006) point to repeated reminders that interventions that seek solutions solely in the efforts of the new arrivals and fail to address the concerns, attitudes and opportunities of the established populations are less likely to succeed. Successful action by local agencies to mediate between new and settled communities is a critical factor in avoiding community tensions, but effective practice is not yet widespread (Robinson and Reeve, 2006).

This matter is also addressed in the final report of the Commission on Integration and Cohesion (2007). Some commentators contend that dissatisfactions are fuelled by sections of the press that continually present refugees and asylum seekers as criminals and/or scrounging off the state (Colville, 2006; Greenslade, 2005; TUC, 2003; Waddington, 2005). Anecdotal evidence to the NIACE ESOL inquiry suggested that negative public perceptions of asylum seekers also engender nervousness in national and local politicians. This affects the level of services and resources they are prepared to allocate to this group.

A recent Refugee Council study found that 75 per cent of respondents had been tortured, 82 per cent had mental health issues and many suffered illness or disability resulting from the effects of war, torture and persecution:

> Flashbacks to war or torture are commonly experienced by asylum seekers and made worse by daily challenges such as racism, employment difficulties and cultural conflicts. The experience of isolation can also result in depression, insomnia and anxiety. Asylum seekers may spend sleepless nights suffering and worrying about dispersal or deportation. (Refugee Council, 2005a, p. 24)

This has implications for learning and support as stress and anxieties can impair memory and concentration and reduce ability to learn.

Women often experience additional discrimination, and have particular difficulties that are often overlooked (Dumper, 2002; Home Office, 2001; Refugee Council; 2005b). Women with male partners have relatively little autonomy as the male is usually deemed the principal applicant. In these cases, the decision on the male's application automatically applies to the woman, and if they separate she is at great risk of becoming both stateless and destitute. Female refugees and asylum seekers, in particular lone parents, can be very isolated. They are often separated from their families or spouse, and childcare responsibilities can limit their opportunities for social interaction.

Women living alone or with children have restricted access to health and other support services, especially if they lack language skills. Females are also more vulnerable to violence and abuse (Dumper, 2002; Kofman, 2005; Refugee Council, 2005b). Many live in fear for their safety, and some endure domestic violence. As many as a third of women refugees have been verbally or physically abused and rarely go out through fear of harassment or abuse. The majority of newly-arrived refugee women live under what Dumper describes as a 'self-imposed curfew', locking themselves inside their homes every evening.

Despite the difficulties faced by asylum seekers and refugees of both genders, we are reminded that it is important not to pathologise them as helpless victims. They are often highly resourceful, skilled and resilient individuals with potential to contribute a great deal to society (Refugee Council, 2002) especially if they can acquire the English language proficiency they need to empower them to do so. As noted earlier, migrants, including many refugees and asylum seekers, bring a wealth of attributes, skills, qualifications and employment experience that they contribute to the economy, the cultural and social fabric of the nation and the communities in which they live (Kirk, 2004; Refugee Council, 2002; Waddington 2005).

The majority of refugees were either working or studying before leaving their country of origin (Aldridge and Waddington, 2002; Bloch, 2002; Kirk, 2004). However, education and employment histories vary significantly between individuals and different countries of origin, covering a spectrum that ranges from individuals with no previous education history at one end to very highly-qualified graduates from professional occupations at the other (Kirk, 2004). Overall, males are more likely than women to have been economically active, although again levels vary between countries.

Data relating to English language skills demonstrate the complexity of defining English language fluency in meaningful ways and the consequent difficulties of quantifying demand for tuition. Bloch (2002) for instance found that on arrival only 17 per cent of asylum speakers reported they spoke English fluently or fairly well while the remainder spoke English slightly or not at all. The picture changes dramatically when country of origin or gender is taken into account. Kirk (2004) noted that refugees from English-speaking countries such as Zimbabwe considered themselves to be proficient in English even when it was not their first language. The Refugee Council (2005a) found that 63 per cent of men claimed to be proficient in written and spoken English while most women said they had limited understanding of written and/or spoken English.

Studies have consistently found that refugees and asylum seekers are eager to work but encounter massive obstacles when trying to enter the labour market (Aldridge *et al.*, 2005; Bloch 2002 and 2004; Hurstfield *et al.*, 2004; Refugee Council, 2002; Waddington, 2005). Bloch (2004), drawing on data from the Labour Force Survey to compare the labour market experiences of minority ethnic groups and refugees in Britain, concludes that refugees are more likely to be unemployed. Asylum seekers do not have the right to work until a decision is made on their status, and many endure lengthy waits for a decision. On gaining their status, refugees are expected to work, but experience considerable difficulties in gaining sustainable employment commensurate with their skills, experience and career aspirations. Like other learners, some refugees are caught in a benefit trap because the rules require them to be available for work and not to study for more than 16 hours a week. Moreover they can be forced to accept low-paid work which means they are not able to undertake full-time training or voluntary work (Aldridge *et al.*, 2005; Waddington *et al.*, 2005).

Other reasons rest with employers (Hurstfield *et al.*, 2004, Phillimore *et al.*, 2006; Waddington, 2005). While many are committed to employing a diverse workforce, others are prejudiced, reluctant to take on people not fluent in English, unaware of the potential of refugees as employees or worried about contravening legislative requirements relating to their employment. Missing certificates and lack of references can restrict opportunities as refugees are often used as a pool of unskilled labour but not considered for a wider range of posts. As a result of this prejudice, muddle and ignorance, the skills and potential of refugees are often squandered.

## Migrant workers

Migrant workers are not a new phenomenon. People have travelled to the UK from other parts of the world for employment for many centuries (Winder, 2005). Like the Pakistani workers recruited in the 1950s to remedy severe labour shortages in the manufacturing sectors

(Tackey *et al.*, 2006), overseas workers are still actively recruited to the UK labour market (Evans *et al.*, 2006; TUC, 2003). The UK government encourages economic migration, recognising that migrant workers make a substantive contribution to the economy and provision of public services by relieving labour shortages and skills gaps, thereby increasing productivity (Home Office *et al.*, 2006). As Evans *et al.* (2006), in their research on migrant workers in the South West of England point out, migrant labour also generates a significant amount of revenue through taxation.

Migrant workers originate from many different countries, within and outside of the European Union, and there is considerable diversity of occupational and language skills within this group. The European Union was enlarged in May 2004 to include the eight Eastern European accession states, known collectively as the A8 states. Nationals of these states have free movement of labour in the UK, and this has led to a huge increase in migrant workers from Eastern Europe (Home Office *et al.*, 2006). Employers' perceive cost and productivity benefits of employing overseas workers as they report that migrant workers are enthusiastic, hard-working and productive employees (Evans *et al.*, 2006; Zaronaite and Tirzite, 2006; Hurstfield *et al.*, 2004). Moreover, as Zaronaite and Tirzite found in their study of migrant workers in South Lincolnshire, they constitute a highly flexible source of labour that can be brought in on a casual basis at relatively low cost to meet seasonal fluctuations in production, 'They are highly motivated, don't miss a day, do exactly what's asked and don't complain' (2006, p. 31).

The tendency to use the term migrant worker to refer to all adults living in the UK for employment purposes masks the fact that they are not a uniform group. On the contrary, although the research base into the characteristics of migrant workers is thin (Evans *et al.*, 2006), the indications are that their backgrounds, status, living and working situations differ considerably. The information that is available usually draws on statistics from the Registered Worker Scheme (Home Office, 2006). This source is limited in that it does not track work and education histories or include data for all migrant workers, but it does provide a useful indication of some trends.

There are substantial regional variations in the number of workers employed in the different sectors (Gilpin *et al.*, 2006; Home Office *et al.*, 2006; TUC, 2003). The type and status of work undertaken by migrant workers covers a huge range from unskilled to professional. In the health and care sector, for example, we can see migrant workers employed as highly-paid doctors and dentists at one end of the scale and in unskilled, low-waged manual or care occupations at the other. Low paid and low status work is more common. Information on the profile of migrant workers (Home Office *et al.*, 2006) indicates that approximately 80 per cent of registered workers earn only £4.50– £5.99 per hour and around half are in temporary employment. This is unevenly distributed across sectors; approximately 70 per cent of migrant workers in the agriculture sector, for instance, are in temporary employment but the reverse in hospitality and catering. The migrant work force is relatively young, with 82 per cent aged between 18 and 34. Work is also stratified by gender, with women concentrated in care, health and education sectors.

Migrant workers are highly vulnerable to exploitation (TUC, 2003). Many employers do value their migrant workers and treat their workforces fairly. However, pay and conditions vary significantly, and many are exploited by unscrupulous employers, agencies or gang masters who disregard their obligations in relation to employees' rights such as the minimum wage, sick leave, working hours and health and safety at work. Workers have little redress because official complaints can result in dismissal or revoking of their work permit, making their position illegal (CAB, 2004; TUC, 2003). This is illustrated by the plight of the rising numbers of female sex workers who are trafficked then trapped in conditions of extreme exploitation (Kofman *et al.*, 2005).

Poor English language compounds migrant workers' problems by hindering their ability to communicate at work, and restricting their knowledge of rights, trades unions and how to seek redress for exploitation. It also affects their ability to comply with the law, communicate with service providers and build relationships in their new communities. Zaronaite and Tirzite (2006) found that English language skills did not improve with length of stay unless there had been a concerted effort to improve them, indicating the vital need to provide English tuition for the workers who need it.

Overall, legal protections for this group of workers have been described by the TUC (2003) as 'wholly inadequate'. Few are union members so lack the protection of trade unions. Moreover, in some workplaces they are vulnerable to prejudice or resentment from peers where they are perceived as undermining established pay, conditions and health and safety. While some workplaces and communities are welcoming, the presence of migrant workers can be a source of tension, especially where the established population and new migrants struggle to adapt to the new cultural circumstances. Heath and Cheung (2006) discovered that prejudice, although dropping over time, has risen again in the past two years. They found high levels of self-reported prejudice against black and minority ethnic groups; 38.2 per cent in transport and communication industries, 36.5 per cent in construction and 36.3 per cent in the manufacturing sector.

There is a paucity of research into the impact of migration. Emerging evidence is indicating that, despite anecdotal evidence to the contrary, the increase in migration from the A8 countries has not resulted in overall higher levels of unemployment or lowered wages (Evans *et al.*, 2006; Gilpin *et al.*, 2006; Home Office *et al.*, 2006). However, the labour market is far from static and the effects of migration on UK workers might play out in different ways in the future, with variations between regions and localities relating to different factors. Migrant workers contribute significant tax revenue and make very few demands of the welfare system (Home Office *et al.*, 2006). In spite of this, myths abound that asylum seekers and migrant workers jump housing queues, receive state handouts, suppress wages and take jobs. Greenslade (2005) in his analysis of the coverage of asylum in the UK press concludes that these beliefs are often fuelled by negative media stories.

We do not have national information on the numbers of migrant workers who leave the UK. Indications are that the majority leave, but we know that a proportion will take up long-term residence. Fifty-three per cent of migrant workers in Lincolnshire, for instance, say they want to stay permanently (Zaronaite and Tirzite 2006). However, intentions can alter over time, and there are likely to be variations between ages, occupations and regions. There are indications that family-related migration is becoming increasingly common, usually women and children joining male migrant workers. As research on family migration has been limited (Berkeley *et al.*, 2006; Kofman *et al.*, 2005), the information available about the skills and participation in the labour market of women who join their spouses is partial. Families place demands on public services, and some areas lack the resources to offer an adequate response. The level of demand for English language from families is unknown, but it does have implications for planning provision. Family members from outside the EU do not qualify for state-funded provision and restricted income prevents many from accessing fee-paying courses (DfEE, 2000).

## Learners living in rural areas

Atkin *et al.* (2005) in their study of literacy, language and numeracy provision in rural areas found that the number of adults in these localities wishing to access ESOL provision has increased rapidly in the last few years, with particular demand from asylum seekers dispersed to rural areas and migrant workers. Developing English language skills can promote settlement, but particular challenges face those wishing to access ESOL provision in rural areas as well as organisations wishing to provide it. Atkin *et al.* (2005) question the extent to which the challenges faced in rural areas are adequately addressed in policies based on urban experience contexts.

New arrivals to rural areas where there is no history of developing services for speakers of other languages face problems in accessing information, advice and other services. They might also experience isolation and encounter difficulties settling into communities with no experience of immigrants. Remoteness tends to reduce their opportunities to attend appropriate English language provision. Providers tend to be reluctant to run classes in areas where the population is sparse and scattered as numbers are insufficient to make discrete ESOL classes economically viable. Travel to larger sites is expensive and time consuming for both teachers and learners, but especially for the poorest who do not have their own transport in areas where public transport is non-existent or expensive and limited (Atkin *et al.*, 2005; Audit Commission, 2007).

This means that learners are often placed either in mixed-level ESOL classes with few progression opportunities, or in adult literacy classes where teachers are not always equipped to respond to all their language needs (Atkin *et al.*, 2005). Different challenges face migrant workers in areas where demand has increased substantially. A lack of experienced, qualified ESOL teachers and insufficient funding constrains capacity to expand the English language offer. Workers also experience difficulties accessing classes as rural employment is characterised by transience, long hours and shift working that prevents regular and sustained attendance. We will return to this question in relation to ESOL for work in Chapter 4.

## Implications for provision

The above has identified some of the characteristics of English language learners. However, as almost all commentators, including Baynham *et al.* (2007), Dalziel and Sofres (2005b), Pitt (2005) and Ivanič *et al.* (2006) remind us, groups are not homogeneous. There is a huge amount of diversity as well as commonalities within and across groups and a spectrum of needs and expectations. Learners bring diverse cultural, educational and employment backgrounds, skills, life histories and experiences. Their circumstances affect both what they want to learn and where and how they want to learn it. They have many different motivations for learning English, and rarely want English for a single purpose, although they often express specific aspirations and priorities within their general aims. These are often related to English to help them to gain work or progress in employment, but the prospects of improved access to services and opportunities to participate in community, cultural and political activities are also important incentives.

Differential educational backgrounds and language skills matter because factors such as length of time in the UK or first language literacy are significant for progress and achievement (Baynham *et al.*, 2007). Adults with little literacy in any language and lacking study skills from previous experience of formal education make slower progress and require more intensive and different kinds of support than individuals with high levels of education and literacy skills in other languages. Learners who already hold educational qualifications tend to seek provision that enables them to make rapid progress. Despite this, an Iraqi professor of engineering, a Somali refugee with no experience of schooling, a Czech builder and an older Pakistani woman with no educational or work experience, might all be learning alongside each other in the same class.

On the one hand this can create interesting groups with rich internal resources and potential for peer support. On the other, we need to ask to what extent do current models of provision provide an adequate response to learners' numerous and disparate priorities, attitudes, skills, learning styles and expectations. Writers such as Baynham *et al.* (2007) and Ivanič *et al.* (2006) point to the challenges of trying to respond to the diverse and complex needs and priorities of different individuals learning in the same groups. Baynham *et al.* conclude that, notwithstanding teachers' best efforts to differentiate learning to meet different needs within their groups, it is virtually impossible to satisfy all learners' diverse needs in heterogeneous classes. If we really want to put learners at the heart of learning and respond to their priorities and learning needs, we need to acknowledge these challenges and formulate a range of different and appropriate curriculum responses and pedagogic practices. Some of these questions will be addressed through an exploration of the nature of ESOL provision in the next chapter.

# 4 What is ESOL?

The diversity of ESOL learners is clear, and responses to demand for English language tuition play out differently in different towns, cities and rural areas. At the same time, there is a strong unifying element. Learners rarely want to learn English for its own sake, but are usually seeking a tool to enable them to do something else, 'The majority of trainees do not want to study English for its own sake; they want to reach self-determined goals that require English'. (Roberts *et al.*, 1992, p. 20). Does ESOL allow them to do so?

The centralised ESOL infrastructure introduced by *Skills for Life*, and the diversity of learner needs, coupled with demographic ebbs and flows and the consequent changes in demand have led writers to question whether current ESOL offers an adequate response. Studies such as Barton and Pitt (2003), Barton and Papen (2005) and Roberts *et al.* (2004) ask whether the ways in which provision is organised and current pedagogic practices meet all these diverse learner needs in ways that take account of their differing histories, expectations and learning styles. ESOL is highly determined by factors such as government targets, the *Skills for Life* infrastructure, funding levels and organisational capacity (Hamilton and Hillier 2006). These affect the type and amount of provision offered and how it is organised. This creates inherent tensions within the system, as learners' priorities do not always align with the government priorities and targets that determine what is funded. As a result they cannot always find provision that fully satisfies their preferences for content, level, duration and intensity (Dalziel and Sofres, 2005a; Evans *et al.*, 2006; Schellekens, 2001).

At the same time, the borders of what counts as ESOL provision have become more fluid (Barton and Pitt, 2003) as the flow between ESOL and EFL, between discrete ESOL and ESOL embedded in other subjects, and between ESOL and adult literacy has altered. Learners pursue their goals in different types of formal and informal settings that include colleges, community venues, the armed forces, workplaces, schools and prisons. They develop their proficiency in English in designated ESOL programmes, or within other subjects in what has become known as embedded provision (Casey *et al.*, 2006; Eldred, 2005; Roberts *et al.*, 2005), and some attend adult literacy classes. This chapter will consider the consequences and implications of the above in more detail in relation to provision. After considering underlying theory, EFL, embedded learning, literacy and ESOL for adults with disabilities and learning difficulties, it will examine ESOL and work, citizenship, and social justice.

## ESOL learning

Consideration of underlying theory can illuminate the development of ESOL policy and pedagogy. Pitt (2005) suggests that although researchers attempting to understand second language acquisition (SLA) have rarely focused on adult ESOL, the conclusions and concepts of this body of research have resonances for pedagogic practice. Writers such as Breen (2001) recognise the complexity of the process of acquiring a second or other language. They suggest that in order to gain a full understanding of language acquisition, research-ers must consider both the cognitive and social aspects of language learning; in other words mental processes, classroom experiences and the social practices and contexts of language use. This entails crossing the boundaries of different disciplines, but as Pitt (2005) notes, a common critique of SLA research is that one of these perspectives is usually dominant and it fails to take sufficient note of other aspects. Early SLA research focused almost exclusively on cognitive processes but more recent studies adopt broader perspectives that recognise the significance of the social nature of learning (Barton and Pitt, 2003; Pitt, 2005).

Recent research theorises well-established practitioner knowledge about ESOL teaching and learning as a social practice view of language use and learning (Barton and Pitt, 2003; Ivanič and Tseng, 2005; Ivanič *et al.*, 2006; Pitt, 2005; Roberts *et al.*,1992; Roberts *et al.*, 2004). It stresses that concepts of language as merely acquiring a set of clearly-defined, decontextualised linguistic skills, which individuals either do or do not possess are too narrow. There is a recognition that language learning is necessarily about acquiring the linguistic elements of the language. This is accompanied by a complementary stress on the ability to use language to communicate in real-life contexts, as theory is informed by the recognition that language cannot be separated from the cultural, social and communicative contexts and power structures in which learners acquire and use it.

If language learning is about enabling adults to carry out the linguistic and cultural interchanges they need to live in a society, it follows that developing technical linguistic skills needs to be integrated with an understanding of societal institutions, structures and cultures and how to operate and negotiate within them (Barton and Papen, 2005; Ivanič *et al.*, 2006). Thus, different groups of learners might have common needs relating to technical language skills, but the contexts in which they apply them might differ considerably. Linguistic transactions and interactions are a product of personal experience, attitudes and cultural conventions as well as linguistic competence. Consequently, they can break down if those taking part are unaware of, or do not conform to, these expectations. This results in misunderstandings, communication breakdowns or reinforcement of negative stereotypes. Many language learners, especially those who are in low-paid or manual occupations, or asylum seekers or refugees, can be trying to communicate in encounters in which there is a significant power differential and where the interlocutor is not necessarily sympathetic (Barton and Pitt, 2003). This can compound communication difficulties. Pedagogic practice, therefore, is strongest when informed by an understanding of the circumstances of learners' lives and the contexts in which they learn and use language.

The extent to which the above understanding has informed the construction and implementation of the ESOL elements of the *Skills for Life* infrastructure is unclear (Hamilton and Hillier, 2006). ESOL straddles the curriculum areas of *Skills for Life* and language teaching but does not align wholly with either. The linguistic theories and pedagogy of language teaching are almost entirely absent from *Skills for Life,* and the social and cultural and political elements influencing language acquisition and use are often missing from modern foreign language teaching. The location of ESOL in organisational structures is not fixed. Evidence given to the NIACE ESOL inquiry (NIACE, 2006) indicated that where ESOL is viewed primarily as a language learning activity it is usually placed in departments with English as a Foreign Language and/or other foreign languages to facilitate interchanges of theory and professional practice. Other organisations place it in *Skills for Life* departments. Language support is often located within support departments and separated from ESOL. This raises the question of how well the distinctive aspects of ESOL are recognised and reflected in either pedagogic practice or organisational and management structures.

## ESOL/EFL

Traditionally ESOL was seen as distinct from English as a Foreign Language (EFL). As society has become more global, migration patterns have changed and learners' interests and purposes have converged, the demarcations between EFL and ESOL have become less distinct and increasingly irrelevant. This section draws out some of the differences and similarities between ESOL and EFL learners and provision.

In the past the division was based on a view that the learners were different and therefore had different needs (Barton and Pitt, 2003). EFL learners were in England for a short time to learn the language for study or work but not with the intention of becoming permanent residents. In contrast, ESOL was characterised by lower-level survival English for learners who had settledin the UK (Schellekens, 2001). The two groups of learners were also differentiated through the presumption that their educational histories differed; EFL learners were assumed to be more educated. EFL is often taught in their home countries using similar programmes to those offered by international language schools so learners tended to be clear about what type of English language tuition they were asking for. In contrast, immigrants requiring ESOL were believed to have rudimentary or no schooling. Hence different theories, methods, and materials were developed. EFL and ESOL were usually offered in separate provision leading to different sets of qualifications (Barton and Pitt, 2003) in which EFL was fee paying and ESOL free. Most language schools offered only EFL, and ESOL and EFL programmes in colleges were often located in different departments and taught by unconnected staff teams.

In practice there was also overlap, particularly at higher levels where EFL materials were used for ESOL, and learners were offered the opportunity to access EFL awards. Many ESOL teachers gained EFL teacher qualifications, and some teachers moved between the two areas. Writers such as Barton and Pitt (2003) suggest that as the demographic profiles of learners have changed, the needs of learners have converged. Thus the borders between EFL and ESOL are no longer either clear cut or as relevant, because the educational and employment histories, motivations and aspirations of ESOL learners now often coincide with those of traditional EFL learners.

This has clouded the differences between ESOL and EFL. Materials designed for EFL are commonly used in ESOL classrooms, and the pedagogy interchanged (Baynham *et al.*, 2007). However, this is not always in learners' interests. Case studies in Roberts *et al.* (2004) demonstrate that materials designed for EFL are not necessarily relevant to ESOL learners' interests or the socio-economic contexts of their lives, especially if not used in ways that engage and interest them to support effective learning.

Current thinking about the importance of learner centeredness in teaching and learning processes (ALI/Ofsted, 2001) indicates that learner interests, purposes and needs ought to determine the type of provision offered rather than an irrelevant EFL/ESOL divide, funding streams or residence status. Some organisations are starting to respond by differentiating courses in terms of learner intention. They offer, for example, structured fast-track courses designed for learners with developed language learning and study skills who want to gain entry to the employment market or higher level study in as short a time as possible. Other courses offer a slower pace for learners with lower levels of literacy or less well-developed skills for learning. However, the evidence indicates too that often the only offer is part-time generic courses that do not cater for the full range of learners (Evans *et al.*, 2006; NIACE, 2006; Rice *et al.*, 2004; Schellekens, 2001; Waddington, 2005). Organisational capacity, the availability of teachers and funding often determine whether organisations are able to provide a full range of differentiated opportunities to respond to the priorities of all.

## Embedded learning

Designated ESOL provision is only one route to developing English language proficiency. Many adults prefer to study other subjects because their main interest is in pursuing wider goals, interests and purposes, often related to employment, citizenship or further study (Eldred, 2005). The range of curriculum areas where this learning takes place is almost limitless, and it is offered in workplaces, communities, and family learning schemes as well as college-based vocational, accredited programmes. As learners' language skills can affect their success in these subjects, it is important to develop their English at the same as the primary curriculum area. This can make a powerful contribution to the equalities agenda by securing inclusion and success in mainstream activity for learners at risk of facing barriers to participation.

As Rosenberg (2006) reminds us, language support was developed in the 1980s when a large amount of innovative work was developed, notably in the ILEA and Shipley College. Although there is little evidence of current initiatives drawing on this work, it could still provide useful reference points. *Skills for Life* appears to have stimulated revived interest in this area of practice, and the term *embedded learning* has been adopted to describe approaches to developing literacy, language and numeracy skills within and as an integral element of another learning programme (Casey *et al.*, 2006; Eldred, 2005). This is still known as language support in some institutions (DfES, 2004a; Eldred, 2005).

Development to date has been fragmented (Casey *et al.*, 2006), and embedded ESOL or language support is not always offered, even by those with a large cohort of learners with language support needs (Roberts *et al.*, 2004). Moreover, the Inspectorates have judged support in vocational provision to be frequently inadequate (Ofsted/Ali, 2003; Ofsted, 2005b). In Ofsted's judgement, learners who wish to access vocational or other subjects too often encounter subject teachers who are both unaware of how language issues affect learning and untrained in how to make their curriculum accessible to language learners.

Eldred's (2005) introduction to embedded practices and a more recent larger-scale quantitative study into the relationship between embedded literacy, numeracy and ESOL and learner retention and achievement by Casey *et al.* (2006) make a convincing case for embedded learning. However, as Casey *et al.* (2006) acknowledge, this research does not prove a direct causal connection between embedded techniques and learner progress and achievement. We do not yet know the answer to questions concerning the extent to which successful learning is a product of embedded language development, and what could be attributed to other factors. Furthermore, we cannot be sure that their conclusions apply equally to literacy and ESOL as these studies do not fully disaggregate findings relating to literacy and ESOL and specific ESOL traits are not identified. Notwithstanding these caveats, the evidence we have to date indicates that embedded ESOL has potential to support successful learning.

A number of research studies have identified different models and success factors (Casey *et al.*, 2006; Dalziel and Sofres, 2005b; Eldred, 2005; Roberts *et al.*, 2005). A common conclusion is that there is no one fixed model of embedding. English language can be totally integrated within subject teaching, linking directly to subject matter and tasks. Other approaches offer bolt-on language support. This is usually designed to relate to learners' specific programmes, but can take the form of generic English language skills development sessions not related to any particular subject. Casey *et al.* (2006) concluded that models where the support was fully integrated with the vocational subject were most effective, helping learners stay the course as well as achieve their aims and qualifications. Although, as noted earlier, the authors also recognise that multiple factors contribute to success, the research clearly indicates that language and subject learning can be mutually reinforcing, and learners become more motivated as they make progress and the relevance of each area of learning is clear.

The process of developing effective embedded learning provision and language support is more complex than merely mapping language skills to the subject curriculum. Supporting learners to develop two sets of skills and knowledge in tandem is a complex process that requires expertise in managing learners' expectations, balancing dual learning goals, devising appropriate pedagogical approaches and materials, and deciding how and when to assess. It requires teachers to work together to devise appropriate approaches and materials that are rooted in an in-depth understanding of how language is situated and used in the contextualised aspects of the programme. In addition it must develop the generic language needed for learning and take learners' attitudes and feelings into account. This might mean developing ways of using spoken language more effectively in teaching (Roberts *et al.*, 2005).

Further challenges, as identified by Roberts *et al.* (2005) in a collection of case studies of embedded practice, relate to the cultural contexts and assumptions underlying the subject material. Teaching materials often place the skills to be developed in a context, for example maths problems presented within a narrative. The aim is to make the material more interesting and accessible to learners. However, it has the converse effect of creating barriers for learners who do not share the linguistic terms or cultural reference frames. As cultural practices associated with vocational areas such as childcare are rarely universally shared, best practice explores different beliefs, traditions, expectations and practices with learners.

Teachers need to clarify boundaries and consider how to balance subject and language skills development. A common finding is that collaborative models in which subject and specialist language teachers work closely together are the most effective (Casey *et al.*, 2006; Dalziel and Sofres, 2005b; Eldred, 2005; Roberts *et al.*, 2005). Although some teachers are specialists in both ESOL and the main subject, it is more common for subject and ESOL experts to work together to develop the learning programme. This is then either delivered through a team approach or solely by the subject teacher. Teachers might need to alter the ways in which they work. Those not used to teaching alongside colleagues have to adapt to collaborative ways of working in classrooms. This can entail modifying teaching styles to ensure that language teachers also have time and space to work with learners in the class. ESOL teachers might have to negotiate and establish their role and relationship with the learners in the vocational context (Casey *et al.*, 2006; Roberts *et al.*, 2005). Casey *et al.* (2006) concluded that positive staff attitudes are as important as structural aspects in successful embedded programmes.

Huge benefits can accrue from collaborative working as departments and individual teachers share expertise to enhance learners' progress and achievement. Effective practice is more likely to be observed where coherent organisational structures, clear strategic leadership and cross-departmental team working are in place to underpin language support and embedded learning (Casey *et al.*, 2006). In addition to developing teachers' skills and knowledge, best practice entails building mutual commitment and respect and establishing mechanisms for communication, and collaborative planning and delivery. Professional development and support to equip staff for this type of teaching is also vital. Subject teachers need to enhance their understanding of the language demands of their subject and learn from ESOL pedagogic practice how to support ESOL learners, and ESOL teachers need to understand the vocational subject matter (Casey *et al.*, 2006; Roberts *et al.*, 2005).

## Literacy development

Reading and writing for adult speakers of other languages is a further area requiring particular attention. As there has been little research into teaching reading and writing to bilingual adults in the UK (Barton and Pitt, 2003), our knowledge about the distinctive features of ESOL written literacy acquisition and development is still immature. As the Scottish Executive definition indicates, a person with limited or no literacy in English can have varying levels of speaking skills and literacy in their first language:

> A person who has little or no literacy in English and who may or may not have literacy in another language and whose spoken English may range from basic to fluent. (Scottish Executive, 2006)

The learning needs of these bilingual adults with limited literacy can be complex and are not always recognised or addressed in either adult literacy programmes or ESOL programmes.

Although the numbers have not been quantified, we know that many bilingual adults do learn in literacy classes. They might choose to do so for a number of reasons; because, like the Caribbean or African heritage learners identified in Chapter 3, they do not identify as ESOL learners, they want to learn alongside English speakers or they feel comfortable with their oral skills and want to focus on other literacy skills. Other learners have no alternative since they want to learn in areas or with providers where ESOL is not offered. This is often the case in community venues in urban neighbourhoods or in rural areas where there are insufficient numbers of adults wanting ESOL classes to make courses economically viable (Atkin *et al.*, 2005).

There are both advantages and potential disadvantages for bilingual adults attending adult literacy classes. They can gain significant benefits from a focus on literacy and the opportunity to interact with English speakers. On the other hand, their specific linguistic development needs are often different from those of native speakers of English, and there can be a detrimental effect on learning where teachers are not equipped with the specialist knowledge to respond (Atkin *et al.*, 2005). The inclusion of both language and literacy in the new teacher education programmes should provide the opportunity to address this. Studies such as Roberts *et al.* (2004) have identified group discussion as an important tool for fostering language development, but we don't yet know enough about the implications of these findings for those learning in an individualised learning environment where there are fewer opportunities for structured talk.

The question of learner literacy also has significant resonance for discrete ESOL provision. Learners range from those with very little experience of reading and writing in their first language to those with highly sophisticated literacy skills in one or more other languages. They encounter difficulties where their reading and writing skills are out of alignment with the dominant level of the group, and their progress can falter or stall as a result. This is particularly true for adults with little or no literacy in any language.

Individual's language profiles often differ so that oracy skills can be more developed than reading and writing skills, or vice versa, and sometimes the language and literacy used in their education is not their primary spoken language. This means that the ways in which they approach learning and the speeds at which they learn can be very disparate. However, differentiated provision is not always available to accommodate the range of needs. Learners who have little experience of literacy in any language can face significant barriers to learning and progress (Spiegel and Sunderland, 2006), and this can demotivate both teachers and learners. These learners' difficulties might be compounded where they have been settled in the UK for some time but have not accessed provision if, as Baynham *et al.* (2007) suggest, long-term residents tend to make slower progress than recent arrivals. Learners without written literacy skills often fail to progress or stay the course because their particular reading and writing development needs are not met. Baynham *et al.*, (2007) conclude that classes where learners with very limited literacy skills are taught with highly literate learners 'cannot be effective'.

A major question is how best to develop the skills of learners who have limited experience of education and little or no literacy in any language. Research does not provide any conclusive solutions to the challenges of ESOL literacy, but a number of studies have started to address this question. Roberts *et al.* (2004) indicate that different methods can be equally successful and popular with learners and that no one approach can be designated correct. Spiegel and Sunderland (2006) in their guide to basic ESOL literacy teaching also advocate adopting pluralistic approaches that draw on a range of pedagogical strategies. For them, like Pitt (2005), ESOL literacy teaching should always be meaningful and relevant to the learners and underpinned by an ethos that promotes learner choice and autonomy.

Adults with well-developed oracy but less experience of reading and writing tend to find classes at their literacy threshold too basic and undemanding, but struggle in higher-level courses where the literacy demands are too great (Barton and Pitt, 2003). Learners with sophisticated literacy skills in other languages might also find that they have to come to grips with unfamiliar cultural assumptions and conventions in written English (Pitt, 2005). At the same time their contextual and cultural knowledge can provide a rich resource for literacy learning although this is not always drawn on in positive and creative ways to enhance learning (Roberts *et al.*, 2004).

There is a small amount of UK research to suggest that using bilingual staff and teaching strategies can bring about successful literacy learning (Barton and Pitt, 2003). Pitt (2005) cites studies from America to suggest that bilingual approaches that draw on the oral and cultural understanding of the learners to bring about successful learning. However, as Barton and Pitt (2003) note, the UK studies often lack evidence of pedagogic practice or omit to explore in any detail the relationship between bilingual approaches and other factors that might also have had an influence. Developing our understanding of these processes could significantly enhance practice.

A further question concerns organisation. Baynham *et al.* (2007) and Dalziel and Sofres (2005b) observe that it is especially difficult to develop literacy skills in the group environment, especially in mixed-level classes. They conclude that these learners might benefit from separate intensive programmes or supplementary individual tuition. Overall, we still have insufficient knowledge about this area of learning and more research is needed to help us understand how bilingual learners best learn and advance their literacy skills in both ESOL and adult literacy provision.

## English language for learners with disabilities and learning difficulties

A number of adults seeking English language provision have physical disabilities, learning difficulties or mental ill health. This has profound implications for them as learners and for the institutions providing learning. These organisations need support to identify appropriate strategies to respond, but there is a serious shortage of research, and as yet few robust and consistent mechanisms for sharing practice in this area (Armstrong and Heathcote, 2003; DfES, 2006c). Recent publications have been produced to help to alleviate this scarcity of resources (DfES 2006a and 2006b).

Disability and ethnicity are rarely considered together by organisations representing the needs of minority ethnic or disabled adults. Bodies concerned with the needs of black and minority ethnic groups seldom consider the specific issues concerning disabled members of those groups, and disability organisations often fail to consider factors relating to ethnicity. As a result, Bray (2004) and DfES (2006c) suggest, individuals have been isolated and excluded. Furthermore, lack of either pressure or support from these bodies has contributed to the underdevelopment of policy, strategy and practice in many fields, including ESOL.

The issue of disability and ethnicity is a complex area in which there are many challenging issues and questions but few definitive answers. Recently published guidance to good practice in making English language provision accessible to learners with learning difficulties or disabilities is designed to support advances in practice (DfES 2006a, 2006b, 2006c and 2006d). Armstrong and Heathcote

(2003), DfES (2006c) and Maudsley *et al.* (2003) draw attention to the politically and culturally determined nature of disability and the terminology used to describe it. The language, knowledge and assumptions about disability and learning difficulties that inform practice in the UK stem from Western cultural concepts that are not necessarily universal or shared by people from other cultures. Moreover, beliefs are not static but alter in response to changing circumstances, and are also likely to differ within and between different cultures (DfES, 2006c). Consequently, while it is possible to develop general guidance, neither universal solutions nor definitive directions are available.

The above studies show that cultural beliefs and perceptions can influence both how disability is defined and attitudes to disability. In turn this affects the extent to which learners acknowledge or disclose their disability or seek assistance. Views of disability can vary within as well as between different communities and minority ethnic groups. Some do not recognise the concept of disability, or they understand and respond to it in a different way to the Western notions that underpin policy and practice. This lack of shared understanding of disability can compound the barriers created by language and lead to misunderstandings and conflicts of expectations between staff, learners and their families.

Terminology might differ, or there might not be direct translations or shared understanding of terms commonly used in the UK such as 'stress' and 'learning difficulties' (DfES, 2006b; Maudsley *et al.*, 2003). This has profound implications for both communications and assessment of need. Levels of awareness of rights and differing attitudes and assumptions to those prevalent in the UK also affect what happens in learning provision. Teachers need understanding of these factors as well as strategies for navigating this difficult terrain.

Assuming that disability is culturally neutral can lead to responses that fail to recognise different cultural assumptions, attitudes and solutions to living with disability. One example of this is where the autonomy and independence assumed in the social model of disability prevalent in Britain can be viewed as individualist and uncaring or cruel in cultures where family support is both the norm and regarded as a duty (DfES, 2006c). Some professionals' views are founded on inaccurate myths regarding cultural responses to disability, for instance that some cultures 'look after their own' which can lead to inappropriate responses. A layer of complexity is added where the learner's wishes and aspirations are in ˙ conflict with those of their family. Their problems are compounded when language is a further barrier to accessing knowledge about the services available and access to interpreters and translated information (Armstrong and Heathcote, 2003).

The above means that processes for assessing learners and referring them to appropriate provision are fraught with difficulty. Referral might depend on the first point of contact as much as, or more than, a learner's own wishes. Specialists from the separate fields of ESOL and learning difficulties or disabilities do not always have training in assessment skills to enable them to identify need in the other area. Consequently, learners might be referred to designated provision for learners with disabilities and learning difficulties because their disability is the professional's primary perspective. This is problematic where ethnicity and culture rather than disability is the learner's primary identity, and language their immediate learning goal (Armstrong and Heathcote, 2003; DfES, 2006c). A different complication is that language and communication needs can be confused with, or mask, some disabilities. Teachers might not be aware that a learner with little English has learning difficulties, especially where they do not communicate through English and are not referred by an external agency (DfES, 2006c). As a result they might not receive appropriate support and leave their class because of frustrations with progress.

Similarly, dyslexia might not be recognised because it is attributed to language development needs, and this can have a negative effect on progress in language learning (Sunderland, 1997). The quantity of research investigating how dyslexic bilingual adults learn the English language is limited (Barton and Pitt, 2003; Pitt, 2005), although some guidance on ESOL and dyslexia is available (DfES, 2006a; Sunderland, 1997). These texts observe that determining the cause of a learner's difficulties can be problematic as many of the 'indicators' of dyslexia are the same as, or similar to, difficulties that many ESOL learners will experience. There are practical difficulties in providing appropriate support. Specialist dyslexia support staff tend to be adult literacy specialists, so are often inexperienced in addressing the specific learning needs of language learners. Training in this area is minimal for many teachers since this area is not always addressed in specialist dyslexia training. This is compounded by a paucity of resources for assessing bilingual learners. Assessment is difficult without using the learner's first language if he or she does not have sufficient oral English skills to complete assessment activities or to take part in the interview process.

In common with the rest of the learner population, ESOL learners experience mental health difficulties. Arguably, insufficient attention has been paid to this matter in the *Skills for Life* strategy (Hodge *et al.*, 2004). While mental health problems are by no means restricted to refugees and asylum seekers, these learners are especially vulnerable as a result of experiencing trauma, and sometimes torture, in their country of origin. They can continue to suffer anxiety and depression when settling in this county (Refugee Council, 2005b; Hodge *et al.*, 2004), but there is little UK research into the effects of trauma on learning (Barton and Pitt, 2003).

Concepts of mental health are constructed within the context of a particular society and culture (DfES, 2006a). This means that our understanding of what constitutes mental health in the UK is not necessarily applicable everywhere, and what is considered healthy functioning in an individualistic culture where people are encouraged to be independent and self-reliant may be very different from the behaviours expected in more collectivist societies. Furthermore, Western models of mental health care, which have developed in stable and affluent societies are based primarily on talk therapies, and may not always be culturally appropriate. This means that the assumptions of teachers and support workers might differ radically from those of learners. Moreover, talk therapies are likely to be inaccessible unless provided in first languages.

Mental health difficulties can impact on learners' ability to attend classes and to learn so it is important that teachers are aware of appropriate responses and approaches. However, holistic provision in which learning organisations work in partnership with mental health services is uncommon, and there has been little guidance or training for teachers. Although embedded in Community Care policy, practice is very slow to emerge. The notion of personal development through education as a key component in mental health care is embedded in recent policy initiatives and is specifically a feature of the Care Programme Approach but it is taking time to filter through and inform practice on the ground.

Sensitive initial assessment and referral to appropriate provision and support is essential for all learners with disabilities or learning difficulties. Cultural factors add a layer of complexity that can be compounded by language levels and learning needs, creating a complex challenge for developing responsive and inclusive models of English language learning. Teachers and other staff need more than awareness of the issues. They need training to develop their knowledge and expertise in the assessment and teaching approaches most effective to empower learners with learning difficulties or disabilities to meet their language learning aspirations, how to make best use of support workers and how to use technology to support them to learn (DfES, 2006a).

## Work and ESOL

Despite the policy emphasis on skills for employment, many of the solutions to demand for ESOL for work do not fall neatly into DfES and LSC policy priorities, targets and funding streams (DfES, 2005f; DWP, 2006; Leitch, 2006). The final Leitch report (2006) addressing UK skills gaps is virtually silent on the issue of migration, omitting to consider either migrant's contributions to the economy or their English language development needs. The question of how ESOL provision can be developed to enable adult speakers of other languages to realise their aspirations and secure and progress in employment commensurate with their skills and abilities is timely. Work is often the most effective site for learning for employed adults, but workplace ESOL brings significant organisational and funding challenges. ESOL for work and employability is hugely important but a complex area in which a number of tangled issues are in urgent need of resolution. What is the curriculum, how do we organise it, how do we train staff to do it and how and who should pay? This chapter will consider some of the barriers facing settled and recently-arrived migrants entering the UK workforce before discussing pre-employment and workplace ESOL provision.

## Migrants and work

The desire to develop English language skills related to work contexts is common to adults from settled communities, refugees, asylum seekers, and migrant workers. Many workforces are diverse so that, for instance, Portuguese women, older Pakistani women who have lived in the UK for many years, Polish migrant workers, and Kurdish refugees could be found working together on a production line. Often university professors, doctors, engineers and mechanics will be working alongside them because bilingual adults from skilled or professional backgrounds often struggle to secure and progress in work to match their qualifications, skills and experience. Reasons for this include regulations relating to immigration status, difficulties achieving recognition of their qualifications by UK professional bodies, benefit requirements, employers' expectations, prejudice and, not least, lack of access to provision to develop English language alongside the other skills and knowledge they need for work.

As well as language skills, many refugees and asylum seekers experience problems gaining recognition of overseas qualifications or tracing qualifications as they lose certificates when they have to leave in a hurry. Gaining higher-level qualifications to prove English language competence to employers is difficult and expensive. Limited awareness of recruitment practices, lack of UK work experience and knowledge of UK work practices constitute further barriers (Hurstfield *et al.*, 2004; Waddington, 2005). The catalyst for long-settled residents might be change of employment forced through redundancy as jobs in declining sectors disappear. Focused support could help unemployed second-language speakers since evidence indicates that the probability of securing employment diminishes with the length of time they are out of work. Women are particularly likely to feature in this group as gender-related issues such as caring responsibilities and cultural expectations often affect their participation in the labour market.

## English for employability

Newly-arrived and unemployed adults frequently aim to acquire the skills and knowledge they need to help them secure work. Asylum seekers do not have the right to work while their claim is under review, and this can affect morale and motivation (Yai *et al.*, 2005). Opportunities to study can provide purpose and support during the waiting period and help to prepare for entry into the labour market. This is particularly important as applicants are expected to become economically active as soon as they receive notice of a successful claim and at this point many feel forced into low-paid work. Language proficiency can help individuals to realise their aspirations and potential, and help them to reintegrate into their home labour markets if their application fails.

Some learners will enter vocational programmes, highlighting again the importance of language support. Many adults wanting to obtain work have to access discrete English language provision, usually generic everyday or survival English, which does not correspond with their employment-related aims. Evidence gathered by the NIACE Inquiry (NIACE, 2006) indicates that there is insufficient provision relating to employment. Few programmes offer intensive tuition with sufficient hours and the range of levels required to meet needs (Bloch 2002, Employability Forum, 2004; Schellekens, 2001; Waddington, 2005).

English language tuition can be needed at all levels from very basic to advanced level 3 or 4, but *Skills for Life* only funds free ESOL provision up to level 2 and from September 2007 will only offer free provision to adults in receipt of means-tested benefits. Writers such as Schellekens (2001) have found that skilled professionals seeking opportunities to develop the higher-level language skills they need for access to suitable employment or progression to higher-level study often encounter obstacles. Expense, and lack of provision in some areas, are barriers to taking up qualifications such as IELTS (International English Language Testing System). This can further inhibit people's opportunities to train to work in their original profession. It is a particular obstacle for health workers where eligibility to work is conditional on gaining a high IELTS score. This could be viewed as making little sense in the policy context developing in response to reports such as Leitch (2006) that assert that building a workforce with higher-level skills is critical to building a high-skill economy and achieving long-term prosperity.

Language is only one element of the skills and knowledge that many recently-arrived adults need to equip them to work in the UK. Programmes have demonstrated that holistic models that draw together different employment-related elements are a highly effective means of connecting learners to the job market (Waddington, 2005). These approaches are founded on inter-agency working and occupational English language that includes culturally appropriate communication skills to enhance occupational identity and competency. Nurses, for instance, as a case study by Shrubshall and Roberts (2005) demonstrates, need to know what type of communications with patients are viewed as appropriate, as well as the language structures to use. A document produced by the Employability Forum (2004) that explores how to equip refugee nurses to enter the workforce also finds that the IELTS qualification tests language whereas the most urgent need is a focus on oral communication skills for the work environments in which the language will be used.

Lack of the language and cultural knowledge needed to succeed in job application processes can pose a significant obstacle to gaining employment. This is not new knowledge but was recently highlighted by Roberts and Campbell (2006) in research that highlighted ways in which the language demands of job interviews often exceeded the language levels required to carry out the job that the candidates were seeking. A more significant factor than language levels was that candidates were unaware of the cultural conventions of UK interviews and this led to inappropriate discourse strategies and misunderstandings.

Additional work-related components to address these matters could include specialised information, advice and guidance, job-seeking skills, support to convert qualifications, cultural awareness of the cultures and conventions of UK workplaces, work experience and voluntary work placements (Waddington, 2005). Research by Erel and Tomlinson (2005) demonstrated that work experience and voluntary work placements are an extremely effective means of assisting women refugees into work. However, there are as yet few opportunities for pre-employment preparation, including supported volunteering opportunities available, and funding is a huge barrier to development as not all the constituent activities qualify for LSC funding, the major funding source for learning activity. Moreover, integrated approaches to addressing employment preparation are rarely reflected in national or regional policy and planning structures or funding regimes.

## ESOL for workers

ESOL is important for bilingual adults in work, whether they are from settled communities, refugees or short-term migrant workers. Despite the recognised advantages, employees face significant barriers to accessing provision. Long and unsocial hours and shift-working patterns in many occupations leave workers with little time or energy to attend classes (Atkin *et al.*, 2005; Evans *et al.*, 2006), and college or community-based provision is not always available when they are free to attend. The temporary and transient nature of some employment, especially the agricultural work undertaken predominantly by migrant workers further reduces opportunities for continuity in learning. Rural workers might be housed in hostel or dormitory accommodation away from towns and centres where college provision is located.

One solution is to provide English language provision at work. Work is often the best location for this learning as these sites can help to overcome the barriers to access that makes access to ESOL doubly difficult for many workers. Although the level of English required to carry out jobs differs in different roles and occupations, all employees need skills to understand their rights at work as well as to communicate with colleagues and managers who do not speak their language, negotiate conflict situations, and understand work-related instructions and health and safety and other legal requirements. Language skills also build confidence and enhance promotion prospects (DfES, 2004b).

In addition to rewards gained by the learners, considerable business benefits can accrue to employers who support *Skills for Life* provision in their work places. These include increased productivity, enhanced morale and employee retention, saving on recruitment costs, better communications and working relationships (Ananiadou *et al.*, 2003; DfES, 2004b; Payne, 2003; TUC/BSA, 2000). Trade unions make a powerful contribution to promoting workplace learning to both workers and employers (TUC/BSA, 2000), although their reach is limited since many ESOL learners are employed by non-unionised micro businesses and small companies.

Employers' attitudes vary. While some are enthusiastic, others do not recognise that improving language skills can benefit their business, or they believe that training is the responsibility of the education sector. Some rural employers of migrant workers consider that they don't need language skills for unskilled work (Atkin *et al.*, 2005; Dalziel and Sofres, 2005b; Hurstfield *et al.*, 2004). Even where companies recognise the implications for health and safety and quality standards, the solutions adopted are sometimes first-language faced, for example translating essential information or using workers who speak English to lead teams. Sceptical employers tend to be very reluctant to allow paid time off work for training.

These are not new problems, and the approaches developed by Industrial Language Training, which was developed in the 1980s to respond to the needs of minority ethnic workers whose working circumstances prevented them from attending mainstream classes (Roberts *et al.*, 1992), offer lessons for contemporary practice. There was a hiatus in workplace developments following the demise of Industrial Language Training, and there is as yet little contemporary research into this aspect of English language learning (Barton and Pitt, 2003).

The earlier work adopted an anti-racist perspective that located language learning within an understanding of racism and disadvantage (Roberts *et al.*, 1992). Communication at work is vital and there was early recognition in Industrial Language training of the importance of interventions that foster inter-ethnic communication which still holds. This work stressed the importance of enhancing all workers' understanding and communication skills, not just those of the bilingual workforce. As English language is integral to the contexts in which it is used, it was seen as essential to integrate linguistic elements with generating understanding of the cultural assumptions, workplace relationships, discourse conventions and contexts in which communication takes place. Thus any view of workplace language learning as merely occupation-related vocabulary is seen as an impoverished view of language learning that will inevitably result in a limited curriculum. Workers also have wider purposes for language learning, to equip them to make choices, live in their communities and communicate in wider society, which should be reflected in curriculum development.

More recently, models for effective workplace ESOL provision have been developed in many occupations through the Union Learning Fund, ESOL Pathfinder and Train to Gain schemes (Dalziel and Sofres, 2005b; Hillage *et al.*, 2005; TUC/BSA, 2000). The national ESOL Pathfinder projects demonstrated that workplace ESOL is a specialist area of work and that considerable amount of development work is required to establish this type of provision (DfES, 2004b; Ward, 2004). Success has been demonstrated to rest on convincing employers and employees of the benefits, building trust, conducting successful negotiations to design provision that accommodates working patterns, designing appropriate recruitment strategies, often in partnership with union learning representatives, and developing customised language programmes and materials that take account of both occupational contexts and wider learner needs (Dalziel and Sofres, 2005b; DfES, 2004b; TUC/BSA, 2000).

Organisations and their staff must be flexible and able to work in employers' premises at times to suit employees and employers. These are often outside 'normal college hours' and include mornings, evenings and weekends. The work can be fraught with obstacles. Workers in some occupations, often agriculture, are required to be flexible and undertake overtime with little notice. This disrupts learning and is also extremely frustrating for teachers who might travel considerable distances to work to find that all their learners have been pulled out of class to fill an urgent order for cabbages. It is also important not to consider language training in isolation, but to link it into general workforce development opportunities and progression routes. Concerns have been raised that frequently neither workers' nor employers' learning needs align with national *Skills for Life* priorities. Inflexible targets and funding relating to qualifications can be in direct conflict with employers' and employees' interest in non-accredited short courses. In addition, as suggested earlier, qualifications do not reflect the language needs of work environments (JH Consulting, 2005).

## ESOL for social justice and citizenship

The commitment of the current government to bring about greater social equity (HM Government, 2006; ODPM, 2005), has a particular resonance for ESOL learners:

The test of a strong and fair society is whether the most vulnerable can thrive. Thriving in modern Britain means more than 'just getting by' – it means living a life with prospects, dignity and a sense of control. That is our aspiration for everyone and we have helped many people to achieve it – e.g. by raising educational standards, lowering pensioner poverty and reducing fear of crime but it is not yet a reality for some of our most disadvantaged citizens. (ODPM, 2005, p. 2)

This is not yet a reality for many ESOL learners, especially refugees and asylum seekers. They experience complex material, legal, social, physical and health circumstances, are often socially excluded and live in poverty in marginalised communities (Robinson and Reeve, 2006; Zetter *et al.*, 2006). All are vulnerable to discrimination and racism, and different aspects of their lives are entwined so that developments in one area impact on others. While language development in itself is neither the cause nor full solution to complex and mutually reinforcing disadvantages, enhancing language skills can help to make a massive difference to whether or not they thrive. This section will draw out factors relating to the social exclusion of many ESOL learners, the relationship between language and social inclusion, and the potential of ESOL to enhance inclusion through specific initiatives: ESOL for citizenship, family learning, community action and offender learning.

English language continues to be one of the most significant factors in successful settlement because language proficiency supports individuals to gain control over their lives, make informed choices, secure employment, communicate, access support and services and develop knowledge of their rights (Home Office, 2005a and 2005b; Phillimore *et al.*, 2006). Language development can also assist adult speakers of other languages to gain the skills they need to obtain citizenship, contribute to the communities in which they live and combat the racism and prejudice that some unfortunately encounter. This potential can be enhanced where social justice and citizenship concerns are embedded in ESOL programmes (Barton and Papen, 2005; NIACE and LLU+ 2005) and approaches that foster learner control and autonomy are adopted; for instance the Reflect democratic participatory approach to teaching and learning described by Archer (2005) and Lopez (2005).

## Social exclusion and language

It is widely recognised that while people from Black and minority ethnic communities are from diverse backgrounds and are represented in different socio-economic groups, they are still most at risk of living in poor circumstances in disadvantaged areas, disproportionately concentrated in low-paid employment, in inferior housing and in poor health (Robinson and Reeve, 2006). Many refugees and asylum seekers, for instance, are housed in emergency, poor standard accommodation, often for up to a year (Refugee Council, 2005a), and need additional services such as health and social care. They are frequently unaware of either the availability of services or their entitlement to access them. Migrant workers can be relatively well paid, because of their occupation or because they work long hours, but still share the experience of poor housing and access to services. Women often face additional problems, but there has been little research into gender and migration and this matter has been relatively neglected in policy making (Kofman *et al.*, 2005). These disadvantages can be multiplied when poor language skills limit access to employment, health care, services and rights.

Established populations living in poor communities also experience these disadvantages. As a result, new migrants can be viewed as competition for already scarce resources or as jumping the queues to gain access to them (Greenslade, 2005; Zetter *et al.*, 2006). Discrimination and racism is prevalent in some areas, and public and government opinion have seen links between immigration and social disruption and sometimes terrorism (Berkeley *et al.*, 2006). There is often little understanding of the circumstances that prompt refugees and asylum seekers to flee wars and persecution, or economic migrants to leave their homes and families to seek work. Instead of encountering understanding, they can be confronted by racism, antagonism and resentment.

Greenslade (2005) offers a powerful exposure of the ways in which this is fuelled by negative media coverage that stokes up prejudice and hostility by encouraging beliefs that refugees, asylum seekers and other immigrants are responsible for endemic social ills such as poverty, crime and shortages of decent housing. In some areas fear and racial hatred are stirred up by the activities of extremist groups (Greenslade, 2005; Home Office, 2001 and 2005b). Greenslade also maintains that anti-Islamic feeling has strengthened, inflamed by fear of terrorism and hostile press coverage of 11 September 2001, the London Bombings in July 2005 and events in Iraq. The *Daily Express* front page on 27 July 2005 illustrates this:

> Bombers are all sponging (sic) asylum-seekers – Britain gave them refuge and now all they want is to repay us with death.

In these circumstances, the ESOL class often becomes a refuge or safe haven (Hodge *et al.*, 2004), and many ESOL teachers become committed champions of their learners' rights (Hamilton and Hillier, 2006). Opportunities to liberate learners to build the language skills and knowledge they need to access services and take action for themselves to improve their circumstances are woven into many language programmes. Others develop a specific focus on activities to bring about greater inclusion and this will now be considered in relation to ESOL for citizenship, family learning and community action.

## Citizenship

The disturbances in Northern England in 2001 brought community tensions to public attention and precipitated a debate about integration. The Home Office responded by establishing a review led by Ted Cantle to investigate factors affecting community cohesion and make recommendations for action. The review group observed a deep polarisation in some towns and cities where members of different communities live 'a series of parallel lives' in which they rarely, if ever, come into contact with others (Home Office, 2001). Robinson and Reeve (2006) remind us that new arrivals do not inevitably fracture community relations and the consequences of immigration in local areas differ. Reactions depend on a range of factors such as the perceived background and identity of the new arrivals, socio-economic dynamics, and the previous history of immigration to these communities. Studies have consistently shown that there is most prejudice against 'foreigners' from people who have least contact with them (Zaronaite and Tirzite, 2006; Colville, 2006; Robinson and Reeve, 2006; Zetter *et al.*, 2006).

Government solutions have been located in policy to build cohesive communities in areas of high immigration (Home Office, 2005a and 2005b; Commission for Integration and Cohesion, 2006 and

2007). The activities of far-right groups are to be curtailed. Measures have been proposed to support settlement, participation in civic society, cross-cultural understanding and foster a sense of common belonging through an increased commitment to citizenship (Home Office, 2005a and 2005b). Analyses such as Zetter *et al.* (2006) characterise this as a marked departure from the previous policy discourse of multiculturalism, which is becoming labelled in some areas of government as a 'challenge to national identity'. Policy rhetoric retains a pluralist vision of communities that supports the acceptance and celebration of difference, multiple identity and promoting shared aims and belonging. However, Zetter *et al.* suggest that in practice the ethos has become much more assimilationist through the promotion of citizenship and national identity. Notions of identity and what it means to belong are complicated, as people have multiple understandings, as seen in current debates on the meaning of Britishness. Lack of English language is clearly identified as a barrier to integration and developing English as one of the solutions (Commission for Integration and Cohesion, 2006 and 2007)

Citizenship is now enshrined in legislation. The Nationality, Immigration and Asylum Act, 2002 requires United Kingdom residents seeking British citizenship to be tested to show 'a sufficient knowledge of English, Welsh or Scottish Gaelic', to have 'a sufficient knowledge about life in the United Kingdom' and to take a citizenship oath and a pledge at a civic ceremony. Sir Bernard Crick, led an advisory group on how this could be put into practice, and the government accepted most of the ensuing recommendations (Home Office, 2003). The requirements for citizenship are that applicants whose English is at Entry Level 3 and above must take the new citizenship test, but do not need to take a separate language test. Applicants who have not yet reached Entry Level 3 in English will be able to meet the requirements for citizenship by successfully completing an ESOL with citizenship course that uses approved learning materials incorporating information about life in the UK. In 2005, it was announced that applicants for settlement will also have to satisfy English language requirements (Taylor, 2007).

The benefits of citizenship include the right to apply for a British passport and travel outside the UK. The system can be seen as offering equal access to legal citizenship for learners who have had very little previous education, and have low levels of literacy in any language. However, the initiative is too young to have generated research-based evidence of the demand it has created for language provision or of the longer-term impact and benefits of ESOL for citizenship for participants.

## ESOL and family learning

ESOL family learning programmes are promoted by government as an important means of bringing about greater social inclusion (DfES, 2005d). Current policy and practice foregrounds the importance of parental involvement in children's learning and, increasingly, in participating in shaping and planning activities in childcare organisations and schools (DfES, 2005b and 2005d). They maintain that family learning makes a powerful contribution to children's educational achievement as well as providing opportunities for parents to develop their own language skills. Anecdotal evidence and case studies such as Rees *et al*. (2003) provide persuasive testimonies to the value of ESOL family learning, as does research carried out by NFER for the Basic Skills Agency (Brooks *et al.*, 1999). However, the consistent evidence-based research that could illuminate the most effective models and pedagogical practices is sparse.

The quest for effective ESOL family learning is important. Parents' and carers' language skills can affect the level of access and influence they have in childcare and education organisations, as well as assist them to support their children's care and education. This could make a difference to the large numbers of children from black and minority ethnic families who fail to reach their full potential at school (Home Office, 2005a). It is even more pertinent if research findings that connect children's under attainment in schools to parents' literacy skills (Bynner and Parsons, 1997 and 2006) also apply to bilingual adults with little English. It is impossible to conclude this with any certainty however, as the extent to which ethnic differences override class and economic status is not known in relation to these findings. School achievement is not consistent across different cultural groups. Children from Pakistani, Bangladeshi, and Black African backgrounds achieve below-average GCSE results whereas children from Chinese and Indian backgrounds achieve GCSE results higher than those of the population as a whole (National Statistics, 2006). Research by Carneiro, Meghir and Parey (2006) does indicate that one of the significant factors in children's education is the level of the mother's education, and family learning is an important means of raising whole family achievement.

ESOL family learning is often provided through the national Skills for Families programme, funded through the LSC. These programmes aim to develop parents' language skills, enhance their ability to help their children and boost their children's language acquisition. The guidance also stresses the importance of celebrating cultural practices and using first languages to support learning (DfES, 2005b).

Many schools have developed in-depth understanding of their pupils' cultures and their parents' views on education. They respond in ways that respect diverse cultures while developing parents' confidence to participate in school life and support their children's learning. In other schools, Gregory (1996) contends, misunderstandings arise between school staff and bilingual parents and carers, often stemming from contradictory cultural expectations of the function of schools and roles of parents in education processes. Bilingual parents tend to recognise their lack of knowledge of the British education system for instance, but at the same time have extremely high aspirations for their children, and often feel that schools have low expectations and don't stretch their children enough. This can be particularly acute where the teaching methods used are so different to those employed in their educational culture that they regard them as play. On the other hand schools expect high levels of parental involvement in supporting children with their learning, and can be frustrated where parents fail to do so, often not realising that these parents regard academic development as the school's responsibility and their role as nurturing and caring. Language skills can also inhibit some parents.

Writers such as Blackledge (2006) and Gregory (1996) have found that parents are often highly active in pursuing their children's development of first languages. Thus, they suggest, changes in school practices to recognise and develop bilingual parents' capacity to help their children can do a great deal to accelerate progress. This is particularly important in the light of recent research by Kenner (2007) that concludes that bilingual learning can provide substantial benefits for children. Family learning can assist teachers, parents and carers to negotiate these cultural boundaries. This can be of enormous help to schools, especially those with no experience of this work striving to work with new communities of refugees, asylum seekers and migrant workers. It can also provide accessible entry points to learning for the women who are otherwise excluded from English language tuition.

Support for children and families, especially those living in poor areas, includes Sure Start Children's Centres which support disadvantaged families with young children. One challenge they face is to ensure that children from black and minority ethnic families benefit. This has particular application for ESOL as bilingual and multilingual parents are often unaware of services or the benefits they can offer, or they experience inappropriate provision.

Every Child Matters is the government's overarching strategy to provide better and more integrated services for children, and to develop the children's workforce to underpin implementation (HM Government, 2004). Recruiting bilingual staff to this workforce will ensure that it reflects the cultural plurality of society and enriches the experiences and outlooks that services offer to children. These staff can act as role models and offer valuable bridges and cultural translations between childcare organisations, schools and homes. They can help raise aspirations and contribute to furthering positive community relationships. ESOL provision can foster development opportunities to equip adults to secure employment in this important occupational sector. Family learning could provide access points to journeys to prepare for work in the sector but robust evidence to illustrate effective practice in this area is limited.

Extended Schools are being introduced under the Every Child Matters umbrella to offer a wide range of services to children and their parents in the community they serve during an extended school day. These services include childcare, parenting and adult learning programmes, health and social care support services, and after school activities. A fundamental principle of their development is consulting with parents and involving them in planning (DfES, 2005d). Ensuring that bilingual families are active in these processes will enrich whole school communities, and at the same time help them to accord value to all the cultures and languages of their communities and avoid the imposition of dominant cultural values. ESOL family learning can help learners acquire the skills they need to take an active part in transactions such as consultative arrangements and to influence the ethos and organisational aspects of school and childcare provision as well as helping their children to thrive and succeed.

## ESOL for community leadership and activism

Bilingual adults can develop language skills to support them to become active in their communities and speak out against prejudice and racism. To reiterate a point made earlier, many bilingual adults are resourceful individuals who are able to survive adversity. Some will possess the skills and aptitudes to become the community leaders, activists and social entrepreneurs that are needed as grass roots change agents in renewing and developing sustainable communities.

Many migrants are experienced political and community activists and trade unionists. Indeed some sought asylum because of their political activities, and it should be recognised that for this reason they may wish to avoid any type of activity that could jeopardise their safety in the UK. On the other hand, there is potential to support interested learners to build on their skills to contribute resource and credit to communities and workplaces (Refugee Council, 2002). They can, for instance, participate in democratic structures, and undertake community activist and leadership roles. The possibilities cited in DfES (2005e) include membership of community organisations, tenants groups, or action groups working to improve neighbour-hoods, becoming a school governor, organising or helping children's sporting activities or acting as community representatives on Local Strategic Partnership groups. The Commission on Integration and Cohesion (2007) has also stressed the importance of language in building communities.

Zetter *et al.* (2006) suggest that fluency in English, coupled with other skills for leadership are highly important for building social capital, but observe that some community leaders are not proficient in English. Language development can be addressed through ESOL classes, although embedding it in wider capacity building might be of most value to both individuals and their communities. Critical approaches such as Reflect, that draw on the ideas of Freire (1972) to link language learning to processes for liberation and action might be particularly relevant for this type of provision (Archer, 2005; Lopez, 2005), not least because they could provide a framework for critical reflection on contested concepts such as community cohesion, citizenship, identity and Britishness.

However, the Reflect approach is not widespread in the UK, although widely used globally. Moreover, there is little in prevailing DfES and LSC discourses to prompt language learning for community activism, although building community capacity is a central concern of other departments and policies (Home Office, 2005b; ODPM, 2003, 2004a and 2004b; SEU, 2004). It is possible that it might acquire greater significance in the light of policy moves to ensure a greater role for citizens in shaping local services. Greater and more effective community engagement, for instance, is a key theme that threads through the debate on the future role of local government. In reporting on a comprehensive review of the role of local government, Lyons (2007) emphasises that local authorities must genuinely engage with and listen to local people. Developing language skills will be critical to the success of these processes.

## ESOL for offenders

Offenders from black and ethnic minority communities comprise approximately 25 per cent of the prisoner population of England and Wales (DfES, 2005c). Although precise figures are not available, inevitably a proportion will be adults with English language development needs and, as in the wider population of ESOL learners, their English language fluency, education and employment histories will be very varied (Dalziel and Sofres, 2005a). Other than the ESOL Prison pathfinder, which investigated ESOL provision for offenders (Dalziel and Sofres, 2005a), there is little research into ESOL provision in custodial settings, although the generic research findings do carry some messages for ESOL.

Developing literacy, language, numeracy and vocational skills and qualifications is claimed to make a vital contribution to supporting offenders to gain sustainable employment, integrate into their communities and stop re-offending (DfES, 2003b and 2005c; Uden, 2004). Despite this, offenders face significant barriers to accessing education, training and employment, and these are more acute for those with English language development needs (Braggins and Talbot, 2003; Dalziel and Sofres, 2005a; Uden, 2004). These obstacles are inherent in the current system. While there are some very committed teachers and creative and inspiring teaching (Dalziel and Sofres, 2005a) there are also serious concerns about poor quality of provision where learners experience inadequate assessments of need and progress, and uninspired utilitarian teaching supported by inappropriate materials.

Speakers of other languages serving sentences in prisons where there are small numbers of ESOL learners are offered only literacy or mixed-level ESOL classes that do not fully meet their needs. Moreover, both teachers' and learners' efforts are frequently undermined by prison regimes (ALI, 2004b; Braggins and Talbot, 2003; Dalziel and Sofres, 2005a; Ofsted/ALI, 2003; Uden, 2004). Learning in prisons is regularly disrupted as sessions are cancelled or learners are transferred to different institutions. Braggins and Talbot (2003) found that learning is paid at a lower rate than work and this can act as a disincentive. Prison officers influence take-up of learning and this varies as their attitudes range from positive to hostile. Dalziel and Sofres (2005a) concluded that there would be substantial benefits in upgrading ESOL in prisons. Offenders serving sentences in the community also frequently experience difficulties accessing appropriate, high-quality provision (ALI 2004b; Dalziel and Sofres, 2005a; Ofsted/ALI 2003).

The problematic aspects of learning provision for offenders are being tackled by a radical change in the organisation of offender learning and skills. The Learning and Skills Council has assumed responsibility for planning and funding all learning and skills provision for offenders and is working in close partnership with the National Offender Management Service, National Probation Service and other partners to bring more coherence to offender education and training across custody and community settings (DfES, 2003b). Offenders' access to learning, including ESOL is to be enhanced through interventions that include staff training, improving initial assessment processes and ensuring cohesive learning journeys as they serve their sentences. A government Green Paper (DfES, 2005c) identifies a need for substantial reforms, and the regenerated system aims to provide more coherent support for the offender's learning journey in which the primary destination is to be employment. Thus the focus will be on enhancing skills and motivation, with the intention of supporting reintegration into community and family life and preventing re-offending. Providing ESOL for offenders and ex-offenders to help achieve these aims is a challenge that has not yet been consistently resolved in either custodial or community settings.

This chapter has shown that as learners' backgrounds are very diverse and their motivations and priorities for learning extremely wide-ranging, different sorts of responses are needed. Learners develop language skills in discrete ESOL, adult literacy or embedded provision. The content is frequently generic language skills but might also have a specific focus or purpose such as developing language and cultural skills and knowledge needed in workplaces, schools and communities. Current theory emphasises that, as effective practitioners have always known, the linguistic aspects of language learning cannot be separated from the social, cultural and economic contexts in which language learners use language. The next chapter will discuss how this plays out in teaching practices, learning and support.

# 5 Teaching, learning and support

The quality of teaching and learning is a recurring theme in ESOL. Rosenberg (2006), in her article charting the role of the National Association for Teaching English and other Community Languages to Adults (NATECLA) in ESOL, notes that there has been awareness of good quality alongside poor practice for at least 25 years. The best ESOL, whether in discrete language classes, language support or embedded programmes, is creative and inspiring and enables learners to realise their aspirations. The inspectorates have noted some outstanding practice of this nature in recent years (ALI, 2004a and 2005; Ofsted, 2005b). However, the overall picture painted of discrete and embedded ESOL and leadership and management is one of variable quality, with too much uninspired and ineffective teaching, and shortcomings in assessment processes, management, leadership and support (ALI, 2003; ALI, 2004a; Grief and Taylor, 2002; Ofsted/ALI, 2003a; Ofsted, 2005a and 2005b).

A core curriculum, common assessment processes, materials and a suite of nationally-approved qualifications for teachers and learners have been developed to support the implementation of *Skills for Life*. These developments are intended to support improvements in the quality of teaching and learning; a major strand in both the *Skills for Life* strategy, and *Success for All* (DfES, 2002), the national strategy that aims to sharpen the focus and improve the quality of all post-16 provision for education and training. The quality of learners' experiences and achievements are also central elements of the *Common Inspection Framework* (ALI/Ofsted, 2001). Why, then, does mediocre and poor practice appear to have persisted as ESOL quality frameworks have been put into place? Is it, for instance, a consequence of inherent problems in the underlying philosophy and content of these frameworks; is it because the infrastructure has not been in place long enough to make a difference; is it a consequence of the rapid expansion of the workforce; or are there other underlying reasons?

At the heart of the debate about quality is the question of what constitutes effective pedagogic practice. The research base that could help us answer this question is somewhat sparse, as ESOL pedagogy for adults is relatively under-researched in the UK (Barton and Pitt, 2003; Ivanič and Tseng, 2005; Pitt, 2005). Recent research studies, for example those carried out for the National Research and Development Centre for adult literacy and numeracy (NRDC) and summarised by Mallows (2006) are starting to redress this and advance our understanding of effective pedagogical practices that support learners to progress and achieve their goals.

Several themes and questions recur in this literature. The first is that ESOL teaching and learning processes are extremely complex and multifaceted. Thus the notion that any one teaching method or approach will suit all learners is inaccurate and unhelpful (Baynham, *et al*. 2007; Ivanič and Tseng, 2005; Roberts *et al.*, 2004). Other questions concern the extent to which current quality frameworks and processes support ESOL pedagogies that enable learners to achieve all their multiple language learning goals (Baynham *et al.*, 2007; Ivanič *et al.*, 2006; Pitt, 2005; Roberts *et al.*, 2004). Explorations of these themes identify a degree of tension between the current policy emphasis on individual learning and the social and transactional nature of English language learning. This plays out through provision and practice underpinned by the new teaching and learning infrastructure. Some consider this has given a focus to ESOL work and sharpened practice, but for others considerable challenges remain unresolved.

## Curriculum

The national adult ESOL core curriculum, introduced in 2001, provides a starting point for discussion of current ESOL teaching and learning. Opinions of the curriculum are very divergent, ranging from welcoming it as an enabling tool to viewing it as restrictive and narrowing what is taught (Ivanič *et al.*, 2006; Roberts *et al.*, 2004).

The curriculum document sets out language competencies at different levels and is designed to support teachers to assess learners' starting points, development aims, progress and achievements and construct learning programmes.

> The ESOL core curriculum offers a framework for English language learning. It defines in detail the skills, knowledge and understanding that non-native English speakers need in order to demonstrate achievement of the nation standards. It provides a reference tool for teachers of ESOL in a wide range of settings, including further and adult education, the workplace programmes for the unemployed, prisons, community based programmes and family learning programmes. (DfES, 2001b, p. 2)

Teachers' evidence to the NIACE ESOL inquiry (NIACE, 2006) indicated that, following some initial suspicion, the curriculum has been broadly welcomed in the field, although some strong reservations remain. Respondents identified the advantages for teachers and learners of a comprehensive skills framework with standardised skills descriptors for different levels. Many new entrants to the profession regarded it as an invaluable resource that assists them to make sense of how the different language skills and cultural features of language and discourse can be integrated in meaningful ways. Some experienced teachers viewed it as a helpful collation of the knowledge they have built up over time, and a useful guide to what is expected at different levels in the revised accreditation.

The curriculum document (DfES, 2001b) sets out linguistic features in detail and suggests contexts in which they can be developed. Barton and Pitt (2003) note that the curriculum was developed by a group of ESOL experts who drew on their professional knowledge as well as modern grammars derived from a corpus of real life oral and written language texts. This means that it incorporates a large body of language descriptors and skills that encompass those used in many real-life transactions and interactions. Even so, studies such as Roberts *et al.* (2004) find that the full range of language skills actually used by learners at each different level are not fully described. Writers such as Ivanič *et al.* (2006), Papen (2005) and Roberts *et al.* (2004) suggest that there are deep-seated limitations in the extent to which a standardised definition of appropriate language skills can reflect fully the diverse range of individuals' needs.

The curriculum is intended as a framework rather than a prescription for learning (DfES, 2001b). The guidance stresses that the contexts in the curriculum document are intended only as examples and teachers should design the content of their teaching to meet the interests of the learners they are working with (DfES, 2001a). This should provide teachers with the freedom to exercise their professional knowledge to devise learning programmes that integrate the social and contextual elements of language use with linguistic content. Thus the curriculum can be viewed as offering potential for adaptation in meaningful ways that liberate learners and reflect their many and diverse interests and purposes.

This will depend on how the curriculum is used in practice. Julka (2005) proposes in an article in *Reflect*, the magazine of the National Research and Development Centre for adult literacy and numeracy, that the ESOL core curriculum should be used selectively in response to learners' needs rather than followed as a linear programme of study. However, there are indications that it is being used by some practitioners in ways that narrow the learning content. Inspectors have expressed concerns that the curriculum is being used too rigidly and teachers are not adapting and using it creatively to satisfy learners' needs (ALI, 2005). As Baynham *et al.* (2007) and Ivanič *et al.* (2006) observe, in less experienced or knowledgeable hands the curriculum can generate programmes focused on instrumental language skills. These, they suggest, can override the development of the full range of skills and cultural understanding needed for interaction in real life. This might be especially true where accredited programmes based on the national standards are perceived to constrain flexibility to go beyond the curriculum specifications.

A further limitation lies in neglect of the so-called 'soft skills' that enhance learning and progress. Barton and Papen (2005), DfES (2003a) and Dutton *et al.* (2005), identify the importance of building confidence and self-esteem, and developing skills for study and critical reflection for progress in language learning. These areas are absent from the ESOL curriculum, and the research literature is largely silent on effective pedagogic practice to integrate them with language development. Confidence and self-esteem are also abstract and difficult to measure. Learners, however, value them highly. Enhancing personal skills and attitudes has more merit than merely supporting learners to feel good about themselves. They are intrinsically linked to successful English language and literacy skills development (DfES, 2003a; Weir, 2005) as they underpin both the learning process and ability to use new language skills and cultural and social knowledge autonomously in real-life situations (Ward with Edwards, 2002).

## Individual Learning Plans (ILPs)

While there appears to be almost universal agreement that learners should be placed at the heart of teaching and learning, what learner-centred processes should look like is contested territory. Individual learning plans, known as ILPs, have become a somewhat contentious focus of this debate since the *Skills for Life* infrastructure brought about their widespread introduction into ESOL. This sparked a great deal of disquiet amongst practitioners, many of whom, as reported by Mallows (2006), question the value of ILPs for ESOL. Other commentators suggest that learners' personal needs and their development as independent learners can be obscured in group-based approaches to planning and assessing learning. Appropriate processes are needed to provide responses to individual interests, priorities and learning needs in a language learning context (Ofsted, 2005b). Questions then concern whether the ILP models that have become prevalent in ESOL fulfil this purpose.

The reality of many ESOL learning environments is that learners are diverse, and even in single-level groups might have different priorities and interests, and learn in different ways at different rates. As inspectors have observed, the specific needs arising from these differences can be masked in group learning environments, especially where processes to ascertain and respond to personal learning priorities are lacking. They report that too much teaching is insufficiently differentiated to meet learner needs; too complex for learners at lower language levels and insufficiently challenging for more advanced learners (Ofsted, 2005b).

Learner-centred approaches and planning learning to meet individual's needs are viewed as fundamental elements of good practice in post-16 learning (ALI/Ofsted, 2001; DfES, 2003a). They require practitioners to work with learners in order to establish their starting points, aims and aspirations, plan teaching and learning activities, and review progress and achievement (DfES, 2003a).

Appropriate processes to plan learning, and identify and record progress and achievement constitute a potent instrument to ensure that ESOL learners' personal needs and interests are identified and addressed, and that they are empowered to take more control of their learning (DfES, 2003a; Julka, 2005). Evidence to the NIACE Inquiry indicates that many experienced teachers are seriously grappling with the very real challenges of meeting the diverse needs of individual students within large, heterogeneous ESOL group teaching situations. Sunderland and Wilkins (2004) and Weir (2005) remind us in their articles in *Reflect* that working with learners to identify their personal aims, develop differentiated learning and recognise progress is what good ESOL teachers have always done. What is at issue is the ILP processes introduced in many learning organisations.

Although there is no nationally-prescribed model for assessing and planning learning, and no common ILP format, many ESOL practitioners indicated to the NIACE inquiry that managers and inspectors do have particular expectations which are based on the individual learning plan models developed in the adult literacy domain (NIACE, 2006). In brief, these ILP s are intended to be owned by the learners, and the process entails working with them to identify their overall goals and learning outcomes which are then broken down into small steps of achievable learning, known as SMART targets (Specific, Measurable, Achievable, Realistic, Time-related). These are recorded on an ILP form and progress against each target is assessed and used as the basis for further planning. Tensions centre on the extent to which this model is appropriate for ESOL (Hamilton, 2006b; Mallows, 2006).

Many teachers regard the ILP processes and formats they are required to use as inadequate tools for the complex task of identifying learning priorities, planning learning and recognising progress and achievement. They are viewed as not only inappropriate, but so bureaucratic and time consuming that they detract from teaching time and produce little discernible learning gain rather than functioning as a valuable and integral part of the teaching and learning process as intended (Baynham *et al.*, 2007; Hamilton, 2006b; Sunderland and Wilkins, 2004; Weir, 2005). Callaghan, writing in *Reflect*, reflects the views of one group of critics in his representation of ILPs as the product of a flawed, centralised top-down model, arguing that they are 'imposed from above, pedagogically flawed and bureaucratically unworkable' (2005, p. 6). Others are concerned that the ILP approach appears to be trying to impose an essentially individualised learning model on to a subject that requires group pedagogies (Barton and Papen, 2005; Roberts *et al.*, 2005).

Researchers have also questioned whether SMART targets fit with the process of language learning. They contend that ILPs comprised of sequential language items expressed as targets do not reflect the reality of how language is acquired and used (Ivanič *et al.*, 2006; Ivanič and Tseng, 2005; Mallows, 2006; Sunderland and Wilkins, 2004; and Weir, 2005). This is because the notion of language as a linear process in which identifiable skills can be broken down into small separate items that can be expressed as measurable, time-bound targets and learned in sequence is inaccurate. They stress that successful language learning is a more sophisticated process that relies on constant and consistent reworking and revisiting language, and practicing it in varying contexts. This is further complicated as the notion of linear progression does not accommodate the influence of first languages on the acquisition of English which for some learners poses recurrent difficulties in achieving fluency and accuracy in particular linguistic features (Barton and Pitt, 2003). Consequently, describing and measuring progress is highly complex. Moreover, prioritising what is easy to measure to provide evidence can skew provision and limit learners by excluding elements of language and progress that are not so easily measured or achieved within given time boundaries (Hamilton, 2006b; Sunderland and Wilkins, 2004).

Negotiation with learners is regarded as the bedrock of learner-centred practice (DfES, 2003a; Sunderland and Wilkins, 2004). Baynham *et al.* (2007), Julka (2005), and Sunderland and Wilkins (2004) affirm the importance of discussing needs and progress with ESOL learners. Participation in these discussions is a fundamental aspect of the process of enhancing analytical and critical skills and becoming an independent learner. Including ESOL learners in planning and reflection is far from straightforward however, especially if the approach used is inappropriate and the language used too complex.

Mallows (2006) poses the problem of how realistic it is to involve all learners in negotiating their ILPs. Learners are able to articulate their needs differently and take part in planning learning and recognising and recording achievement in different ways and at different levels of depth or intensity at different stages of their personal learning cycles. Attitudinal factors are significant, as learners' expectations of teachers' roles and their views as to what constitutes valid classroom activity can influence their notions of what is right. The idea of taking part in planning their learning might seem strange to some because they regard the teacher as the expert who ought to know what they need to learn (DfES, 2003a). In these instances, learners have to explore why, as well as how, to negotiate their learning. As engagement increases over time, their autonomy as learners and their ability to shape classroom practice to reflect their priorities can be enhanced.

The ability of learners with Entry Level 1 and 2 language skills to participate in an equitable way in negotiating ILPs and participating in review processes using the medium of English can be limited, although bilingual methods have some potential to address this. Schellekens (2004) found that even advanced learners struggle to articulate specific linguistic aims and targets of the type recorded on many ILPs, although they do have clear aims and an overall sense of the direction in which they want to travel. Making processes meaningful to learners, especially those who do not have the language to understand or enter into detailed discussion and recording of their learning needs and aims, therefore constitutes a major challenge, but not one that can be shied away from if the principles of promoting learner choice and autonomy are to be upheld. The teacher's role is to work with learners in ways that accord with their language levels to produce a meaningful learning programme that responds to their aims and priorities. This is hugely challenging and critics argue that the SMART target model is not fit for this purpose.

In addition to the critique outline above is the inherent contradiction between designating an ILP a learner's document and at the same time requiring learning to be expressed as SMART linguistic targets. The terminology is inaccessible and does not reflect how learners think about their learning. Baynham *et al.* (2007), for instance, found little awareness or consensus amongst learners of the purpose and value of their ILP document and little ownership or reported use of it as a learning tool. Learners do not usually express their intentions and aspirations in terms of detailed linguistic goals, and conceptualising progress in relation to discrete language items such as past tense endings disconnects language from use in real inter-actions. They tend to report progress in relation to how they use language to negotiate real-life situations in everyday life outside the classroom (Baynham *et al.*, 2007; Ward with Edwards, 2002).

ILP models that reference a skills framework unrelated to this real-life use of language can divorce language learning and assessment of progress in the classroom from the ways in which language is used in interactions outside (Ivanič *et al.*, 2006; Pitt, 2005). When language is used in social situations, capability varies according to the situation; the more controlled the more accurate. Out in the real world those engaged in interaction do not restrict their language to the carefully-planned language items that learners encounter in ESOL classes. They use unfamiliar language, dialects or accents and might be impatient or hostile (Pitt, 2005). As a result, learners' confidence and competence in language use in real-life situations can ebb and flow. As Ward and Edwards (2002) discovered, methods for capturing the use of skills learned in the classroom in real-life situations are relatively underdeveloped. It is difficult therefore to construct smart targets relating to language use in real situations. On the other hand, creative approaches to planning and recognising progress to meet learners' needs using processes tuned to ESOL can be a powerful instrument to ensure that individual's needs are addressed.

Some commentators have identified rising class sizes and an increase in the volume of paperwork required as a difficulty. They contend that teachers do plan learning but struggle to meet very varied personal needs in classes of 20 or more. They also highlight that many teachers view the time required to manage the paperwork entailed in writing detailed individual plans and recording progress in each session as very onerous with few benefits for learners (Mallows, 2006). Moreover, guidance published by multiple sources offers no consensus on the definition, form, content and process of administering ILPs. It is, perhaps, hardly surprising that practitioners report confusion, conflicting guidance and expectations as well as the imposition of a plethora of recording and paperwork. Writers have also questioned how far the paperwork represents real negotiation and planning activity and asked whether the time spent on recording stifles teaching and significantly reduces time spent on language development activity (Callaghan, 2004; Sunderland and Wilkins, 2004).

Identifying and responding to individual needs in group settings poses a significant challenge, and many argue the ILPs imported from adult literacy do little to resolve it. However, there are potential contradictions between the rhetoric of fostering learner autonomy and empowerment and objections to processes designed to bring this about. What processes then are effective to ensure that individual needs are met within ESOL group contexts? Recent research indicates a great deal of consensus that talking individually, often through tutorials, with students to discover their views on their learning and progress and identify future directions is a valuable tool for negotiating and reflecting on learning (Mallows, 2006). In their practitioner research study investigating learner retention, McGoldrick *et al.* (2007) found that learners appreciated individual attention in class and tutorials, and Baynham *et al.* (2007) also noted that some learners value individual teacher time. Teachers view one-to-one interactions as useful for getting to know their learners to determine the factors that influence what they want to learn, how they want to learn and the support mechanisms to enable them to achieve and progress. The challenge for ESOL is to develop these processes and systems for recording them in ways that are meaningful and beneficial to learners.

## Effective teaching and learning practice

Writers concur that language acquisition is a complex process that is not yet fully understood (Mallows, 2006; Ivanič and Tseng, 2005; Pitt, 2005; Roberts *et al.*, 2004). It follows, as studies such as Ivanič and Tseng (2005) conclude, that there is no simple correlation between what the teacher does and what is learned since teacher input is mediated by a host of other factors that are not always possible to predict. Similarly there are no single definitive answers to the questions concerning the most effective practice for supporting learners to progress and achieve.

The findings emerging from recent research appear to confirm practitioners' knowledge; as ESOL teaching and learning processes are extremely complex, no one teaching method suits all learners or all situations (Baynham *et al.*, 2007; Condelli, 2002; Ivanič and Tseng, 2005; Roberts *et al.*, 2004). Ivanič and Tseng (2005) suggest that it is important, therefore, to develop our understanding of the complexity of what is involved in learning. The multiple factors identified as influencing learning and progress include learners' histories and first languages, expectations and learning styles, classroom dynamics and expectations, and external circumstances, relationships and environments (Barton and Pitt, 2003; Ivanič and Tseng, 2005; Pitt, 2005; Roberts *et al.*, 2005).

Baynham *et al.* (2007) conclude that using a balance and variety of activities with a moderate level of grammar teaching is more significant than any one particular method in promoting learner achievement and progress. They also stress that the teacher's skills and vision are paramount in effective learning, describing ESOL teachers as 'bricoleurs'. In other words, effective ESOL teachers adopt flexible and adaptive approaches. They are skilled in drawing on their knowledge of methods and materials at hand to respond to learners' needs and are able to reflect and elicit learning points out of diverse activities, materials and classroom occurrences. The 'professional vision' possessed by experienced teachers is a central element in their capacity to operate in this manner.

For writers such as Baynham *et al.* (2007) this professional vision is a highly-developed critical and reflective understanding of their subject and the wider context in which it operates. This enables teachers to make critical and informed judgements leading to decisions and action relating to classroom practice. These decisions should take account of the potential gaps between teacher and learner expectations identified in studies such as Barton and Pitt (2003), Pitt (2005) and Ivanič and Tseng (2005) since learners' views of what constitutes teaching affect progress. These views are likely to be constructed by previous experience, so that, as noted in the previous chapter, learners might not initially expect the teacher to engage them in planning learning. Similarly, they might be used to practices such as rote learning that differ substantially from what happens in their ESOL classroom. Making these differing outlooks visible could assist learners to modify their expectations and develop strategies to enhance their learning experience and achievements.

## Group learning

Group learning situations play a significant role in helping to create optimum conditions for learning. Researchers tend to concur that the group is particularly crucial in ESOL because it is essentially a collaborative and interactive activity in which learners develop their language and communication skills through talking with others (Barton and Pitt, 2003; McGoldrick *et al.*, 2007; Pitt, 2005; Roberts *et al.*, 2004). Consequently, studies such as Baynham *et al.* (2007), Ivanič *et al.* (2006), and Roberts *et al.* (2004) suggest, understanding the significance of social relations and the dynamics of social interaction and encouraging collaborative group-learning processes are both crucial aspects of English language learning and a means of facilitating the learning. Fostering affirmative group dynamics and peer support can create the conditions in which learners are more able to develop the skills they need to participate actively in learning processes and reflect critically on their learning experiences and progress (Hodge *et al.*, 2004; Ward with Edwards, 2002). It can also help to boost learners' confidence and this, Dutton *et al.* (2005), Ivanič *et al.* (2006) and Ward with Edwards (2002) have found, contributes significantly to progress in learning.

The ESOL learning environment is a place where communication happens. Roberts *et al.* (2004) stress that 'talk is work' in the ESOL class; talk is both a curriculum area and the vehicle for learning; classroom discourse and collaborative learning activities provide opportunities to practice language to improve fluency and accuracy. Studies such as Baynham *et al.* (2007) and Ivanič *et al.* (2006) find this is particularly effective where teachers provide opportunities for less controlled and more authentic oral communication. Learners can also gain knowledge of the rules and cultural expectations governing social interactions and practice negotiating the rules and boundaries of different social and cultural contexts with peers and teachers (Roberts *et al.*, 2004).

The class environment has been characterised by writers such as Ivanič *et al.* (2006) as a learning community in which the social relationships between teachers, students and peers create a culture of mutual support that promotes successful learning. In addition, important emotional, psychological and social benefits accrue from attending language classes and gaining the support and encouragement of language-learning peers (Barton and Pitt, 2003; Hodge *et al.*, 2004; Roberts *et al.*, 2004; Ward with Edwards, 2002). Attending class can provide purpose, structure and motivation which can be difficult to maintain in the face of pressured life circumstances such as waiting for resolution of a claim for asylum.

Peers can provide emotional and learning support and friendship both within and outside the learning environment, providing a sense of identity and helping to combat isolation (Baynham *et al.*, 2007; Hodge *et al.*, 2004). Attention has already been drawn to the traumatic experiences and difficulties in the lives of many learners. Teachers often consciously create the classroom as a safe, supportive environment in which they gain respite from these pressures (Mallows, 2006). Although specific approaches differ, teaching strategies in such circumstances tend to be broadly based on recognition of the realities of students' lives and backgrounds while approaching potentially sensitive subjects with caution (Hodge *et al.*, 2004; Mallows, 2006).

Collaboration and group work is important for learning. However, as noted above, learners also value talk with the teacher, and a number of studies indicate that learners also require individual attention and space within the group environment. Ivanič and Tseng (2005) note that research has not focused on the ways in which silence and space for personal reflection could support learning, and ask whether the need for this identified by research into school-age learners might equally apply to adults. Ivanič *et al.* (2006) found that learners want to feel that their teachers understand and respond to them as individuals, recognising their personal circumstances, learning styles and progress. Baynham *et al.* (2007) concluded that while collaborative learning activities are an important element of effective practice, they are not in themselves sufficient to ensure learner progress and must be linked to a balance and variety of teaching activities.

## Resources

The quality and content of materials and resources used to support learning have a direct influence on learners' satisfaction, achievement and progress. Researchers have found that this is greater where the materials used are both interesting and relevant to learners (Ivanič *et al.*, 2006; Mallows, 2006; Roberts *et al.*, 2002; Roberts *et al.*, 2004). Thus, they suggest, recognising and drawing on the social identities and the huge wealth of experiences, resources and cultural capital that learners bring to the classroom can enhance learning. In this sense, the heterogeneity of language classes can be regarded as a resource (Roberts *et al.*, 2004). However, this potential can be limited where teachers fail to make use of learners' cultural and linguistic resources, or provide learning materials that do not interest or challenge them sufficiently.

Condelli (2002) found that connecting materials to everyday life, 'bringing the outside in', can make a significant difference to achievement. This is reinforced by other studies, including McGoldrick *et al.* (2007), Roberts *et al.* (2004) and Ivanič *et al.* (2006), which found that learners are interested in the relevance of learning programmes for their everyday needs and for integrating into society at different levels. Most prefer, and are motivated by, authentic texts related to their interests and contemporary issues. Generic text book material is often dull and irrelevant, described by a learner as a 'dead mouse' in Cooke *et al.* (2004). These texts can be narrow and constraining, especially when used in ways that stifle discussion related to learners' lives and interests. Chapter 4 discussed ESOL for social justice, democratic purposes and citizenship, and Ivanič *et al.* (2006) and Roberts *et al.* (2004) found that many learners are more interested in these wider social, cultural and political issues than a functional curriculum related to using services. They observe, however, that teachers do not always exploit materials sufficiently to enable learners to draw on their sophisticated level of interests, knowledge and experience to enhance their learning. Learner involvement of this nature is facilitated where teachers are prepared to relinquish their roles as sole experts to enable learners to take more control over selecting topics and texts and determining the content and pace of the class.

## First language as a learning resource

A number of writers propose that the other languages that learners bring into the classroom can be viewed as a powerful resource to assist language learning (Condelli, 2002; Hodge *et al.*, 2004; Roberts *et al.*, 2004; Sagan and Casey, 2005). They suggest that using learners' first languages has a positive impact on achievement. Advocates of using learners' languages stress that it is a positive recognition of their cultures and identities (Pitt, 2005), assists them to feel safe and confident and enables them to express knowledge locked in by underdeveloped English skills. Learners can use first languages to discuss issues relating to language learning; to negotiate learning and assessment, facilitate understanding of the word meanings and grammatical features of English and to assist learners to carry out learning activities (Roberts *et al.*, 2004). This could be of particular benefit in overcoming some of the obstacles to learners with entry-level English negotiating and reflecting on their learning identified in the previous chapter. /

The heterogeneity of most ESOL classes means that learners do not necessarily share first languages. In these cases strategies for working with other languages in linguistically-diverse contexts are required. Skilled teachers, whether they speak the same language as their learners or not, can harness learners' other languages to support learning. They also encourage learners to use each other's languages in collaborative peer learning processes (Hodge *et al.*, 2004; Roberts *et al.*, 2004). Methods include using multilingual oral and written resources, employing bilingual teaching assistants and encouraging learners to speak to each other in first languages for specific activities in class, for example to develop learning plans or to discuss and develop understanding of complex or abstract issues in their own language (Dalziel and Sofres, 2005b; Roberts *et al.*, 2004; Sunderland and Taylor, 2006).

This learning tool is not used systematically in ESOL practice. Belief in its benefits are far from universal and, as Sagan and Casey (2005) note in an article in *Reflect,* many teachers are not convinced of the merits of bilingual learning strategies. The advantages are not immediately evident; providing bilingual support poses logistic and pedagogical challenges and few teachers are trained to use them effectively. Some teachers and learners believe that using first languages diverts attention from English and their use restricts opportunities to develop and practice English. More research and development is needed to advance our understanding of the strengths and limitations of first language teaching methods and inform the development of pedagogic practice.

## Speaking outside the classroom

Language, as noted earlier, has to be constantly reworked and revisited and used in different or more complex ways in various situations. Using language in real settings has been identified as a significant element in becoming a successful language user. Yet many ESOL learners report that they have few opportunities to use English and virtually no social interactions with English speakers outside their ESOL class (Mallows, 2006). Reasons for this include social isolation, working in situations where they use only their first language, being unemployed, and little social contact with English speakers.

This language isolation can be detrimental to progress in language acquisition because, as writers such as Pitt (2005) suggest, there is a positive correlation between exposure to English outside the class and increasing language proficiency. Workplaces, for instance, can provide important informal learning opportunities where adults are able to develop and practice English language skills through participation in social networks. Norton and Toohey (2001) found that social interactions as well as personal characteristics and language learning commitment and skills have a positive effect on progress in learning a language. They point to the difficulties many learners encounter in gaining access to networks where English is used, even in work situations. This highlights the value of classroom activities based on real communication that provide opportunities for authentic language use. For this reason, researchers have noted the impact on learning of taking learners out of the class to use language in real circumstances to supplement classroom activity, concluding that these activities build learners' confidence and advance their learning (Mallows, 2006).

### Assessment and accreditation

Reflecting on learning journeys, recognising distance travelled and acknowledging achievement motivates learners and provides a basis for planning further learning, as noted in the earlier discussion of ILPs. The importance of processes to identify progress and achievement is widely recognised, for instance in DfES guidance to practitioners (2003a) and in the discussion of different perspectives on testing and accreditation in Lavender *et al.* (2004). Debates centre on policy relating to accreditation, the nature of accreditation and the value of the adoption of accreditation as a proxy for achievement in *Skills for Life*. For critics, the target-driven culture prevalent in *Skills for Life* has resulted in an undue emphasis on certification and achievement of a narrow range of qualifications which do not always align with learners' best interests. Hamilton and Hillier (2006: 125), for example, say that 'The distinctions between assessment, testing and accreditation have become conflated in the *Skills for Life* context.'

## New ESOL qualifications

The advantage for policy makers and practitioners of the skills model adopted in *Skills for Life* is that once skills and levels have been determined they can be used to form a standardised basis for curriculum development and benchmarks for assessment. However, what to assess and how and when to assess remain problematic. What is the most appropriate qualifications structure? Should language skills be tested as decontextualised skills, or should they be related to the real situations in which they are used? In other words, to what extent do tests support learners to acquire the language skills they need to communicate effectively in real situations and how well do they assess this capability. Should the acquisition of the so-called soft skills be recognised in some way, and if so how? Which forms of assessment are most helpful and who decides? To what extent and how should learners be involved in assessing their own learning? What happens to learners who don't want to pursue qualifications?

*Skills for Life* has reformed literacy, numeracy and language qualifications, reducing the number of different offers and developing new qualifications to replace them. The rationale for reform was inconsistency in assessment standards, and the confusion created by the plethora of qualifications that had little consistency or cohesion in relation to content, level and quality (DfEE, 1999 and 2000). While some qualifications had gained national and international recognition, the currency of others was limited since many inside the field and even more outside the ESOL world, including employers, had little concept of what they qualified learners to do. Arguably this is still the case.

To address this, new qualifications have been developed, based on the ESOL core curriculum and aligned with the levels defined in the national standards for adult literacy and numeracy; Entry Levels 1, 2 and 3, and Levels 1 and 2. ESOL *Skills for Life* certificates are now available in Speaking and Listening, Reading, and Writing. These have replaced the old qualifications, and now only *Skills for Life* qualifications accredited by the Qualifications and Curriculum Authority (QCA) are eligible for Learning and Skills Council *Skills for Life* funding. While the new consistency has been welcomed, concern was expressed to the NIACE ESOL inquiry about the content of these tests, their currency with employers and education and training providers, and the increasing alignment of certification with funding designed to encourage achievement of Public Service Agreement (PSA) targets.

In contrast to the National Test in Literacy which tests only certain reading skills, an advantage of the ESOL qualification structure is that it offers certification in the four skills of speaking, listening, reading and writing. Learners can follow different pathways, taking either a single mode speaking and listening unit, or an all-mode pathway comprising speaking and listening, reading and writing units. This unitised model is learner-centred in that it takes account of spiky profiles and enables learners to choose to accredit oral com-munication skills separately from literacy skills and at different levels. Learners gain a full qualification when they have achieved units in each of the modes, with a notional 100 hours of learning attached to each.

This model offers huge potential advantages, not least flexibility for the learners, and consistency that supports them to transfer their accreditation more easily as they move through their learning journey. At the same time Qualifications and Curriculum Authority (QCA) requirements and Learning and Skills Council funding and targets are seen by some providers and examining bodies as serving to reduce this flexibility. Although unitisation has potential to offer a more flexible structure, the size of the ESOL units means that a full unit can take learners a long time and significantly more than the notional 100 hours to achieve. Ideally learners would have the opportunity to gain units to recognise stages along the way, but accreditation for smaller units is not recognised by the QCA, thereby restricting opportunities to provide external recognition and valida-tion for smaller chunks of learning. This is an important strategy for motivating learners, and, as ESOL learners are often very mobile, means that they fail to gain credit for large swathes of their learning.

Speaking and listening are wrapped together into one qualification. There appears to be no theoretical rationale for this other than an intention to mirror the structure of the *Skills for Life* standards and curriculum. Listening is a distinct skill and recognised as such in both EFL and language qualifications. This failure to recognise the two distinct skills means there is no parity with EFL or modern foreign languages, and denies learners the opportunity to accredit them separately. Further parity questions lie in comparisons with the National Literacy Test. Literacy learners have to do less to achieve a Level 1 or 2 qualification as they are only tested in reading skills, whereas ESOL learners have to achieve in all four skills. From a learner's point of view the full award is more rounded and appropriate, but it is more costly for the provider, perhaps tempting some to steer learners to inappropriate qualifications to draw down funding as cheaply as possible.

Concerns have been raised in London and elsewhere that frequently neither workers' nor employers' learning needs align with national *Skills for Life* priorities. Gathering evidence to inform the development of the London ESOL strategy, JH Consulting (2005) concluded that qualifications do not reflect the language needs of work environments. Inflexible targets and funding relating to qualifications can be in direct conflict with employers' and employees' interest in non-accredited short courses. At the time of writing new ESOL for Work qualifications are in development to address these concerns and will be introduced from September 2007.

### The influence of targets

There has been a shift in emphasis in implementation of the *Skills for Life* strategy from participation to a clearer focus on achievement of qualifications, with funding used as the lever to bring this about. The strategy (DfEE, 2001a) initially focused on the participation of adults seen to be most in need of skills development, but in the revised strategy (DfES, 2003b) this emphasis has shifted to a more rigid concern with ensuring that all learners progress to achieve Level 2 of the National Qualifications Framework. This can be interpreted as a consequence of the PSA targets that have to show measurable progress, since tests rather than participation are viewed as the most appropriate mechanism for this (Lavender *et al.*, 2004). This has been characterised as a somewhat crude measure as tests only measure a particular set of skills and knowledge that a learner has at one specific time and place. They do not relate to starting points so do not necessarily demonstrate progress made, especially as only one learner test achievement counts towards targets.

The LSC wants providers to shift the majority of their provision to programmes offering the nationally-approved qualifications, both as a proxy for quality and to contribute to achievement of the PSA targets. The change is being managed through the introduction of a benchmark of an 80/20 per cent split between learners working towards nationally-approved qualifications and those not (LSC, 2006a). This decision to use funding as a lever to move the majority of learners into provision leading to nationally-approved qualifications provides a stark example of the tensions that arise between externally-imposed requirements to meet national targets and a commitment to learner demand when this demand does not align with policy priorities.

One view of accreditation asserts that all learners recognise the importance of qualifications, albeit they want to enter in their timescale, when they are ready (Lavender *et al.*, 2004). It is certainly the case that many ESOL learners have an academic background and expect to validate their learning through gaining nationally-recognised qualifications that have currency with employers and education providers. The problem is that the approved ESOL qualifications do not suit all learners. Some need to pursue qualifications outside the *Skills for Life* framework, but inclusion of ESOL in the *Skills for Life* portfolio means that only provision, and therefore accreditation, up to and including Level 2 is eligible for funding. English language learners from professional backgrounds who need high levels of English and qualifications to enable them to enter their professions in the UK, for instance the IELTS (International English Language Testing System) examinations that are mandatory entry requirements for some professions, do not attract *Skills for Life* funding (Waddington, 2005), and not all are in a position to pay for this provision.

Others stress the importance of non-accredited learning (DfES, 2003a; Grief and Windsor, 2002). It can attract hesitant learners (Grief and Windsor, 2002). Some learners fear tests and exams, or have reasons and priorities for learning not related to gaining qualifications. Inclusion will entail ensuring that their choices are also accommodated (Ward and Edwards, 2002). Learners might choose not to enter qualifications. They prioritise learning for a particular purpose and if they have no interest in accreditation often do not stay to take exams. New migrant workers often fit this profile. Learners do not always progress along an even, linear path. They can reach a plateau or sometimes fall backwards for myriad reasons, for instance because physical or mental illness, personal problems, or financial circumstances affect their learning. External assessment is not always appropriate in these circumstances. However, it is generally accepted that it is important for all learners to recognise and reflect on their progress whether or not their achievements are externally certificated.

### Recognising achievement

Whatever the test adopted, there are dangers in using qualifications as a proxy for progress and achievement, not least because they can distort teaching and learning. Recognising what has been learned is of vital importance, but research indicates that this should be about more than autonomous skills and what can be counted by accreditation. Ivanič and Tseng (2005) for instance identify different types of learning that include learning about language, strategies for learning, and social relations. A study by Schuller *et al.* (2004) of the wider benefits of learning provides a powerful demonstration of the benefits of participation in learning for personal confidence and well-being, family relationships, health and social and democratic participation.

Focusing on the summative assessment of an end test can divert attention from the practices of formative assessment which as indicated in the earlier discussion of ILPs are crucially important in motivating learners and supporting planning learning and progress and achievement (DfES, 2003a; Lavender *et al.*, 2004). There is common agreement that learners' views should be included in assessment of progress, and this is intended to underpin ILP processes. This is easier to achieve in ongoing assessment than in external tests although the two are not mutually exclusive. Do we count learners' views of progress against their own priorities or against externally imposed criteria and outcomes?

This leads to the questions posed by Lavender *et al.* (2004) about what type of assessment is 'for' learning, in other words assists learners to learn. Strengthening learners' voices in planning and assessing their own learning is important, and assessment processes have been seen as particularly effective when carried out as collaborative processes involving teachers and learners (Ward with Edwards, 2002). This often happens in a one-to-one dialogue between teacher and student, but group and peer evaluation are also a powerful and valuable means of fostering learner autonomy, reinforcing learning and building confidence. Learners' first languages can be an invaluable tool in these processes.

In addition to increasing their awareness of, and therefore satisfaction with, their achievement and progress, learners' contributions to assessment processes can enable teachers to gain greater understanding of their priorities and the life situations that affect their learning. This includes the ways in which skills and knowledge are taken from the classroom into diverse situations. This is important because, as already stated, achievement for many learners is related to how they can speak out and be heard in real-life interactions (Barton and Papen, 2005; Ward and Edwards, 2002). However, recognising achievement in ways that are meaningful and relevant in relation to real situations poses particular challenges. Teachers are not usually present, the responses of other people affect success, transactions can be difficult and interlocutors are not always sympathetic. Collective interactions are also important but complex to capture (Barton and Papen, 2005; Ward and Edwards, 2002). Articulating gains in wider areas such as enhanced confidence and self-esteem is also valuable (Dutton *et al.*, 2005; Ward, 2002; Ivanič and Tseng, 2005), as these enhance ability to use skills in real life situations, for instance having the confidence to use new language which can bring about further progress.

## ICT

ICT is fast becoming an essential skill in many aspects of everyday life and work (Clarke and Englebright, 2003; Mellar *et al.*, 2004; Moss and Southwood, 2006). It is increasingly required for employment at all levels and has become a critical skill for high-level occupations. It has enormous potential as a tool to enhance language learning. As the ESOL Pathfinder projects demonstrated, it is popular with learners and, when used well, heightens achievement (Dalziel and Sofres, 2005b; DfES, 2005a). However, as Barton and Pitt (2003) found, the use of ICT in ESOL remains an under-researched area and we need to know more about effective learning and pedagogic practice.

ICT can be defined in many ways, and encompasses a huge variety of digital technologies, systems and applications (Clarke and Englebright, 2003; Mellar *et al.*, 2004; Moss and Southwood, 2006). For learners, linguistic competence is critical to success in using ICT. They must be able to comprehend the meta-language associated with technology as well as read and write to access and navigate technological functions and programmes (Clarke and Englebright, 2003). Starting points are very diverse. Many will already have highly-developed ICT skills and need only the language skills to facilitate access, but acquiring ICT skills will pose a greater challenge to learners with little or no prior knowledge and undeveloped literacy skills.

E-learning is a valuable tool for enhancing language acquisition and motivating learners (Moss and Southwood, 2006; Vorhaus, 2006). The ESOL Pathfinders found that ESOL teachers have been enthusiastic early adopters of ICT to support effective teaching and learning (Dalziel and Sofres, 2005b). As the use of ICT in ESOL is becoming more widespread, teachers are developing exciting and creative e-learning approaches, often blended with more traditional teaching ICT can be used to support language learning in both teacher-supported situations and autonomous learning (DfES, 2005a). However, as this is relatively new territory, there is still much to be done to enable e-learning to be fully exploited to gain the maximum benefit for learners (Mellar et. al, 2004). There is active development in this area, for instance the ESOL e-learning materials developed for Adult and Community Learning providers (Moss and Southwood, 2006). E-learning and ICT are often promoted as solutions to the limited access to learning in rural areas, and do have a lot of potential, especially when integrated with other strategies. On the other hand, as Atkin *et al.* (2005) warn, high levels of teacher support and guidance can be needed to make e-learning effective. Consequently unsupported e-learning is not the most effective approach for those who have not yet developed sufficient language skills for independent learning.

Many teachers are not yet secure using technology, anc unconfident or lack knowledge of how best to exploit it et. (Dalziel and Sofres, 2005b). Training and support to equip te. with skills and knowledge of effective pedagogies to enable the. .o use ICT to support language learning is crucial. Clarke (2005) and Hunt (2005) propose that e-learning should be an integral element of both initial teacher training and ongoing professional development, and ICT skills are an important element of the new teaching stand-ards framework. In addition to training, mechanisms need to be put into place to support staff to transfer knowledge gained through training activity into actual classroom practice. ICT teachers need language awareness and training in the approaches for supporting language learners underpinned by an effective ICT skills curriculum (Mellar *et al.*, 2004). The Qualifications and Curriculum Authority (QCA) has developed standards and a curriculum for ICT which should provide an invaluable resource.

## IAG, counselling and support

At all stages of their learning, adult speakers of other languages have very specific information, advice, guidance and support needs. As these needs are frequently complex and acute, providing quality advice, guidance and support services for ESOL learners can be far from straightforward. Immigration status can determine entitlement to state-provided learning provision, and other factors such as employment, health, housing, income, benefits, and legal matters can affect people's ability to join, succeed and progress. It is, therefore, absolutely vital that ESOL learners benefit from appropriate specialist advice, provided by either statutory or voluntary and community sector organisations. However, evidence indicates that ESOL learners do not routinely access formal information, advice and guidance services (CAB, 2004; DWP, 2005; Evans *et al.*, 2006), either because appropriate services do not exist, or where they do, limited awareness inhibits access.

Advisers have a very powerful gate-keeping role as they can influence the life chances of the individuals who consult them about access to learning provision and employment. It is crucial that neither language nor cross-cultural misunderstandings create additional barriers. Entitlements, access and progression routes can differ for settled migrants, refugees, asylum seekers and migrant workers. Their needs are often multidimensional and, for many seeking work securing knowledge of pathways by which they can enter and progress in the labour market is paramount. All need informed and sensitive advice to explore the routes that could either enable them to take up their previous occupations, or identify alternatives where this is not possible. Without this they are more likely to remain without work or trapped in low-paid jobs well below their experience and capabilities (DWP, 2005).

Statutory advice agencies including Jobcentre Plus, nextstep, learndirect, Connexions, and college IAG services have a fundamental role to play in advising second language speakers (Aldridge *et al.*, 2005). Jobcentre Plus is connected to the employment sector. The holistic Connexions approach is ideal in providing the support needed by young refugees to overcome the multiple barriers associated with their situation (Connexions, 2003). The information and advice services of learndirect and nextstep are currently being merged to form a new universal adult careers service in England, working in partnership with Jobcentre Plus. This could provide an opportunity for ensuring these crucial guidance issues are addressed. The National Academic Recognition and Information Centre (NARIC) establishes the UK equivalence of overseas academic qualifications, although this is of limited use as it does not recognise all qualifications and many migrants do not have their documentation. Further Education colleges and adult education services are frequently the first port of call for adults seeking ESOL provision, and are well placed to provide advice relating to a range of vocational as well as language options.

Many speakers of other languages fail to consult any of these advice services simply because they don't know they exist or where and how to access them (Aldridge *et al.*, 2005; Bloch, 2002; DWP, 2005; Schellekens, 2001; Waddington, 2005). When they do reach them, advisors and others, including college admissions staff, do not always have the specialist knowledge to respond adequately, especially to refugees and asylum seekers whose situations are frequently complex. Advisers can make assumptions about background, language levels and learning needs and interests that create barriers (Roberts *et al.*, 1992). Research has also found that inappropriate referrals are often made, for instance to discrete ESOL programmes when learners' aspirations and language levels would make supported vocational programmes more appropriate (DWP, 2005; Phillimore *et al.*, 2006; Waddington, 2005). Statutory organisations are not resourced to provide the sustained and holistic support over long time periods that some learners, especially refugees, need in order to re-orientate their skills and return to their original careers.

Problems are compounded by tensions such as those inherent in Jobcentre Plus programmes where targets to move people into work as quickly as possible sit uneasily with the time needed by speakers of other languages to develop their language skills and take part in vocational skills reorientation programmes or training for new careers. This affects all speakers of other languages, but can be particularly acute for highly-skilled refugees needing intense language development and assistance to gain recognition of their previous experience and qualifications.

The Refugee Employment strategy published by the department of Work and Pensions in 2005 recognises that Jobcentre Plus advisors do not necessarily have the specialist knowledge they need to satisfy the full range of advice needs of speakers of other languages, especially those with highly-skilled employment histories (DWP, 2005). The strategy proposed is for Jobcentre Plus to work in partnership with other statutory and voluntary sector organisations to ensure that all needs are addressed. It is often difficult to disentangle education and skills from wider information, advice and guidance needs as adults can have acute needs in both areas, and wider needs can affect learning. Migrant workers for instance might need access to information about rights at work or housing (CAB, 2004; Evans *et al.*, 2006).

Specialist advice is often provided by voluntary and community organisations, especially those with a specific focus on working with specific groups such as refugees and asylum seekers and a deep reach into communities. There are many reasons why these organisations are successful. The combination of small scale and their enhanced awareness of the barriers and rapidly-changing circumstances faced by migrant workers, refugees and asylum seekers enables them to adapt and evolve to meet specific and changing needs. Staff members possess expert holistic knowledge of the circumstances and needs of minority ethnic communities or groups such as refugees and asylum seekers, and are adept in providing one-to-one sustained support for individuals. They are often very flexible in their approach, and a proportion of staff will often share the experiences of the people they are working with. They might, for example, have sought asylum themselves, and therefore have first-hand knowledge of the asylum process and its impact on people.

These strengths are also the source of their limitations. Voluntary sector workers tend to see themselves as support workers rather than guidance professionals, and identify very strongly with the client group. As guidance is only one aspect of their work, they are unlikely to possess or be intending to undertake guidance qualifications. Furthermore, these workers may receive lower pay than other staff in the IAG sector, despite having some of the most highly-specialised skills sets. Voluntary sector organisations often exist on temporary, insecure funding sources, and their workers are often obliged to manage on a grave shortage of resources when project funding begins to dry up. Voluntary sector organisations have nowhere near enough capacity to comprehensively satisfy the high volume of demand, and funding cuts reduce this supply still further and create further obstacles to the statutory agencies striving to create partnerships with the sector. Community organisations for new migrant workers have been slower to evolve and in areas such as Bradford this has placed heavy and difficult to satisfy demands on established communities (Bradford Central and Eastern European Working Group, 2006).

The need for specialist guidance and support does not disappear on entry to ESOL programmes. The circumstances of many learners, as described in Chapter 2, intersect with and impact on their learning needs; they can, for example, affect learners' ability to attend regularly and to concentrate and progress in their studies. Learners might need advice to resolve practical problems, or referral to support for emotional stress. Referrals can be fraught with difficulty. Some learning organisations do not have the capacity to provide specialist guidance workers, and learners are frequently reluctant to approach yet another face or have experienced inappropriate services so tend to rely on their teacher.

Many teachers are ill-equipped to respond, as they lack specialist knowledge and have limited institutional support and time to adopt this role (Baynham *et al.*, 2007; Dalziel and Sofres, 2005b; Roberts *et al.*, 2004). At the same time, they are committed to supporting their learners and recognise that other sources might be unavailable or inadequate. Consequently, even when teachers appreciate where the boundaries of their work should lie, many take on a support role, often outside the classroom, and frequently in their own time as they recognise they have built up trust with learners who are often vulnerable with few alternative sources of support (Hodge *et al.*, 2004; Roberts *et al.*, 2004). This problem is particularly acute in areas where support services and agencies have not adjusted to the new demands resulting from changed migration patterns. However, teachers pay a price as this work is usually time-consuming, unrecognised, and unpaid. It can be extremely stressful, for instance where they come close to learners' traumas or share the frustrations of trying to get things done through services that are frequently overstretched.

The Refugee Council (2005a) has recognised that the traumatic experiences of many asylum seekers and refugees before reaching the UK, including rape and torture, mean that they have an urgent need for specialist counselling. This need is frequently unmet; they can be reluctant to disclose because of shame, inability to discuss their experiences or because they are not asked. Where they do request help, the support needed is often beyond the reach of college counselling services, but specialist services where counsellors under-stand the cultural backgrounds and experiences of these clients are not always available (Stanistreet, 2004). There are few specialist agencies, especially outside London and major cities, and their resources are limited. Equally, the multi-agency approaches that could help organisations to contribute their individual spheres of expertise to holistic support packages are severely lacking, especially in those areas inexperienced in this work (Roberts *et al.*, 2004).

This chapter has addressed some of the challenges and solutions to providing interesting, creative, relevant and effective teaching, learning, support and advice and guidance to the full range of ESOL learners. Complexity is a common thread running through the different aspects. The skills and knowledge of teachers and others working in ESOL are unquestionably vital to the success of this venture. These will be enriched and deepened by experience and reflection throughout a teacher's career, but effective initial training and ongoing professional development are also essential to provide the context and skills, knowledge, insights and challenge necessary to enhance this experience.

# 6 Teacher recruitment and training

It is widely recognised that the expertise of ESOL teachers is a major factor in language development. It follows that employing sufficient trained and experienced teachers is a prerequisite for providing excellent ESOL. Yet increasing capacity is proving a real challenge in the many areas, as employers experience difficulties in recruiting sufficient qualified staff. Ofsted/ALI concluded in their 2003 report that greater teaching expertise was needed in ESOL teaching. In 2005, Ofsted attributed a slight fall in the quality of ESOL provision in colleges to a continuing shortage of specialist teachers, compounded by the lack of knowledge of language amongst vocational teachers (Ofsted, 2005). Training programmes to increase the supply of teachers and promote the professionalism of the *Skills for Life* sector were developed, but these have not yet had a significant impact and there are worries about their scope and content. Initial *Skills for Life* developments have been superseded by reform of teacher training which is in progress at the time of writing. This chapter will outline the profile of the labour force, discuss recruitment questions, then outline the training frameworks and explore some of the debates concerning initial teacher training and the continuing professional development of teachers already in post.

## The workforce profile

Who are the ESOL teachers? The Pathfinders (Dalziel and Sofres, 2005b) and a study of participants in ESOL core curriculum training carried out by Lucas *et al.* (2004a) indicated that the workforce is predominantly female and the majority are white, although the proportion varies between regions; white teachers comprised 67.3 per cent of the London ESOL workforce compared to 89.9 per cent in the

East of England. Their qualifications vary. Many, but not all, hold a professional language teaching qualification and hold qualifications at level 4 or above, although they can be classified as unqualified in the new frameworks. The majority are employed in further education colleges. Recruits enter the profession through a wide variety of routes, including school and EFL teaching. There is less evidence available of the profile of teachers recruited more recently to staff the rapid growth of ESOL, although the speed of this expansion means that it is likely that a significant proportion of these will be inexperienced and, at least initially, untrained. Lifelong Learning UK has commissioned a study to identify the volume and characteristics of specialist *Skills for Life* teachers. This is still in press at the time of writing, but will provide a more up to date picture when published.

## Recruitment

There is an acute shortage of specialist ESOL workers and this affects the nature and quality of ESOL provision (Dalziel and Sofres, 2005b; Ofsted, 2005b). In urban areas high demand often results in long waiting lists and rationed classes. Atkin *et al.* (2005) found that demand has also started to outstrip supply in rural areas where asylum seekers have been dispersed and populations of migrant workers have increased. Expanding the teacher base must entail finding more effective ways of recruiting and training more teachers. In spite of this, Lucas *et al.* (2004b) suggest, scant attention has been paid to this issue, and they discovered little evidence of identifiable strategies for recruiting new teachers.

Addressing the question of what type of teachers could best create positive learning experiences and drive up quality could provide a constructive starting point. Is it desirable to recruit trained teachers from different sectors and disciplines and train them to transfer their skills to ESOL? Do we need more recent graduates, more men, or more teachers from diverse backgrounds? Do we recruit more bilingual teachers to act as role models for learners, enable students to draw on linguistic and cultural practices to support their English language learning and provide insights and information on the backgrounds and the issues facing learners for professional colleagues?

Attracting new entrants to work in the ESOL field poses a great

challenge (Dalziel and Sofres 2005b), not least because empl
conditions are less than attractive to anyone, especially new g
ates, seeking permanent full-time posts in an identifiable car
structure. The ESOL workforce is characterised by a flexible labou
model in which relatively few teachers hold full-time jobs and there
are few career pathways. Around half of all teachers are employed
on an hourly-paid basis, with many others on fractional contracts.
Some teachers actively choose part-time employment, but this
pattern of working carries few of the benefits or pay of full-time
employment (Lucas *et al.*, 2004a). This undermines the value accorded to, or felt by, teachers, and is likely to account for the huge
turnover in ESOL (Sunderland, 2006). Part time, sessional teachers
have less security of employment, lower status, and fewer opportunities to connect with their departments or take-up development
opportunities. It is harder for them to update their perspectives,
knowledge, skills and awareness of national and organisational
developments. New recruits often don't stay, attracted by the
higher salaries and greater stability of employment in other sectors
(Walker *et al.*, 2000). Costs in time and travel for teachers pose additional
barriers for teachers working in rural areas (Atkin *et al.*, 2005).

Making the profession more attractive by improving employment
conditions could help recruitment. New routes into ESOL teaching are
also needed (Vorhaus, 2006). Prospective new entrants to the profession
can be caught in a double bind. They can't access training without a
degree of experience, but they find it difficult to secure placements
before they have trained since managers, understandably, are reluctant
to expose their learners to inexperienced novices (Casey, 2005). Some
of the solution might lie in pre-service training with supported
placements for new entrants or apprenticeship approaches (Casey,
2005; Ofsted / Ali, 2003; Roberts *et al.*, 2005). At the time of writing pilots
are emerging which could provide models and solutions. There are
insufficient teacher training places in areas of high demand such as
London and some rural areas, further reducing opportunities for new
teachers. There is a scarcity of teacher trainers in many areas of England
(Lucas *et al.*, 2005; Sunderland, 2006) and this is particularly acute in
rural locations where there is little history and accumulated expertise
in providing ESOL and no ready supply of qualified, specialist ESOL
teachers or trainers to train new teachers (Atkin *et al.*, 2005).

ı between the quality of ESOL teaching and of initial and in-service teacher training. ıg Baynham *et al.* (2007), have identified the most crucial factors in effective ESOL ..₅ and continuing professional development are .... to support teachers to develop the vision and skills funda-mental to learners' progress and success. Reforms of literacy, language and numeracy teacher education and all post-16 teacher training have been developing in parallel. Each has implications for ESOL teacher education as they are now set to converge. At the time of writing the reforms are taking shape at a rapid pace. Consequently, it is difficult to portray specific aspects with any degree of certainty as the context is so fast moving, but it is possible to identify broad features of the reforms and implications for the field.

The *Skills for Life* strategy specified that all specialist literacy, numeracy and ESOL teachers should work towards a subject-specific teaching qualification. ESOL subject specifications (DfES/FENTO, 2002) were developed which set out the linguistic knowledge, understanding and personal language skills required at levels 3 and 4. Since September 2003 all new specialist ESOL teachers have been expected to acquire an approved qualification based on these standards and a Certificate in Education (Cert. Ed.) or Post Graduate Certificate in Education (PGCE) teaching qualification based on the FENTO standards for Teaching and Learning at level 4. A study of new literacy, language and numeracy teacher training courses by Lucas *et al.* (2004b) found that different structures were offered, ranging from courses where the subject and pedagogic knowledge were fully integrated, through partial integration, to separation of theory and practice. The former has become the prevalent model for specialist initial ESOL teacher training.

*Success for All* recommended that by 2010 all teachers working in the post-16 learning and skills sector should be trained and qualified (DfES, 2002), and a framework for reform was subsequently developed (DfES, 2004). The new structure requires all new entrants to undertake initial teacher training underpinned by the new generic professional standards. All teachers in the post-16 sector will be expected to enhance and update their skills and knowledge through-out their career. ESOL teacher training will be incorporated in this framework and new qualifications for the initial training of FE teachers will be introduced in September 2007. Vocational teachers who are already qualified will be required to gain the subject knowledge to become ESOL teachers.

### Initial teacher education

The generic teaching plus subject specialist knowledge training structure outlined above is problematic for ESOL. Knowledge of English by itself does not lead to effective practice, and generic training is an inadequate preparation for effective ESOL teaching which uses a specific repertoire of language teaching skills and approaches (Casey, 2005; Hughes *et al.*, 2005; Vorhaus, 2006). The standards developed in 2002 were weighted towards personal language skills and knowledge and contain relatively little pedagogic content. Specialist ESOL teacher education courses integrate the PGCE or Cert. Ed with the subject specialist qualification and trainees learn about ESOL pedagogy from ESOL specialists. Other options enable teachers to qualify to teach ESOL by gaining a PGCE or Cert. Ed on a non-specialist course and access the subject specialist qualification separately. In these cases the acquisition of practical teaching skills to develop learners' language skills was marginalised as teachers could qualify to teach ESOL without any exposure to tuition in ESOL pedagogy by ESOL specialists (Casey 2005, Sunderland 2006). Sunderland observed that teachers emerging from this structure were frequently unable to teach ESOL well, and the majority of trainers in the ESOL field view integrated ESOL specific courses as the most effective approach.

The reform of initial teacher training aims to address the above concerns. The need for subject-related pedagogy in ESOL teacher training has been recognised and courses leading to the new qualifications from September 2007 are likely to integrate the special-ist ESOL and generic components in a single framework. However, the question of how qualified teachers moving to ESOL teaching from other curriculum areas will be supported to gain ESOL-specific pedagogic knowledge and skills remains unclear at the time of writing. These teachers need training in how to teach language in addition to subject knowledge and cultural awareness. Even highly-qualified and experienced language teachers moving to ESOL from EFL can find they are not equipped with the cultural awareness and the pedagogical strategies they need to respond to the challenges of teaching ESOL where they encounter diverse groups and significant differences in learner background, demand, literacy skills, learning styles and rates of progress (Dalziel and Sofres, 2005b).

## ESOL teacher education programmes

Cohorts of trainee teachers are very heterogeneous (Lucas *et al.*, 2004b). Participants arrive from diverse backgrounds, bringing different expectations, experiences, skills, knowledge and qualifications. They encompass recently-qualified graduates, adults from a variety of backgrounds training for a career change and experienced teachers. Their experience, prior learning and understanding of the subject is very varied, ranging from level 2 to post-graduate qualifications. Some trainees have degrees in related subjects such as linguistics whereas others bring no specialist subject knowledge. The experience, needs and expectations of experienced ESOL teachers can differ considerably from those of inexperienced teachers or new entrants. Managing training programmes to reflect the needs of participants with these very different requirements can test trainers.

Balancing subject and pedagogical content, that is what to teach and how to teach it, poses a considerable challenge (Lucas *et al.*, 2005). The generic initial teacher education model assumes that trainee teachers arrive with knowledge of the subject they will teach, for instance childcare or catering. ESOL teachers do not necessarily start with the theoretical linguistic knowledge. ESOL teacher education programmes, therefore, have to support trainees to develop their subject knowledge as well as how to teach it. Identifying the most effective approaches to programme structure and how to integrate and order input relating to theory and practice, is a problem common to all teacher education, but is particularly difficult for ESOL (Lucas *et al.*, 2005). Not only do trainees have to develop their subject knowledge and practical expertise, their differing levels of knowledge and experience mean that their priorities are vastly different. Experienced ESOL teachers have rich pedagogical knowledge so tend to prioritise theory, while new teachers have an urgent need to know how to apply the theory in teaching and learning settings (Lucas *et al.*, 2005). Baynham *et al.* (2007) concluded that both aspects, subject knowledge and subject-specific pedagogy are crucial to effective practice and must be central to teacher-training processes.

In their review of the literature relating to teacher education, Morton *et al.* (2006) stress that teacher training is more than acquiring a set of competences since practice is a complex process that is inevitably influenced by the teacher's assumptions, values and beliefs. It follows from this that training should enable teachers to develop the skills and awareness they need to make these value frameworks and beliefs explicit and to analyse and critique their effects on practice. It was noted earlier that early SLA research has shifted from a focus on cognitive processes and the notion of language as a set of autonomous skills to a social practice view of language learning that stresses that language cannot be separated from the cultural, social and communicative contexts and power structures in which learners acquire and use it. It is therefore important that teachers receive adequate preparation to enable them to understand and respond effectively to the realities and complexities of learner's lives and aspirations and the ways in which these impact on learning, as well as the political contexts in which they are learning and using the language (Mallows, 2006).

Context influences learning. Studies such as Morton *et al.* (2006) find that the most effective teacher training adopts and models the methods that participants will use when they teach. This will give them direct experience of effective teaching approaches and insight into how their learners will experience their classroom practice. Training content also needs to reflect the breadth of settings in which ESOL teaching and learning takes place so that trainees become confident and competent to work in different situations with diverse learner groups. Critical understanding through reflective practice of how to plan and deploy a range of classroom practices to respond to the different circumstances and communicative contexts of learners' lives contribute to the professional vision that Baynham *et al.* (2007) and Mallows (2006) argue is critical to successful teaching. This is built through experience, but also, as Mallows suggests, the expertise of established teachers can be drawn on to lay the foundations through appropriate teacher training.

Responding to the demands of the different teaching and learning environments in which ESOL is offered is a complex and challenging process for which teachers need to be prepared. Research has found that ESOL teacher education courses tend to assume that teachers will be working in an FE environment so fail to include context-focused training that addresses the needs of teachers preparing for work in different settings (Dalziel and Sofres, 2005a and 2005b; Mallows, 2006; Vorhaus, 2006). The majority of ESOL teachers are employed by Further Education colleges, but might then be deployed to work in other settings, and those employed by a range of different types of organisations also need appropriate training. They need to understand the organisational and cultural factors that have an impact on learning in environments such as community venues, schools, workplaces or custodial settings. Workplace ESOL and multi-agency approaches to ESOL for employability, for instance, require a specialist knowledge base and skills set that includes systematic knowledge of local labour markets and sector-specific employment issues, legislation, skills in brokering learning with employers, employers' organisations and unions, and awareness of occupational factors and specific language uses as well as wider guidance issues. Those moving to other settings at a later date can acquire knowledge they need at this stage, providing that training is available. However, participants already working in these settings will be best served if their initial training is relevant to their teaching context.

## Mentoring

Quality teaching practice and mentoring for trainee teachers are crucial elements of teacher training as they have a major influence on subsequent practice (Derrick and Dicks, 2005; Morton *et al.*, 2006). Mentored placements support trainees to translate theoretical know-ledge into practice in a guided environment. However, researchers have noted concerns about the quality and consistency of mentoring arrangements for trainee teachers, finding many instances of insufficient or inadequate support (DfES, 2004a; Derrick and Dicks, 2005; Lucas *et al.*, 2004b; Ofsted, 2006; Vorhaus 2006).

Mentoring, like coaching, is relatively new and there is not yet a common understanding of what the role entails, and this is curtailing the ability of trainees to benefit. In addition, a shortage of mentors means that teacher trainers often struggle to source teaching practice placements supported by high-quality mentoring arrangements. In spite of its fundamental importance, little status is accorded to the mentoring role. Pressures on time don't leave experienced teachers with much space to support trainees, and funding is not available to support organisations to release experienced staff to take on mentoring roles (Derrick and Dicks, 2005; Lucas *et al.*, 2004b). Morton *et al.* (2006) observe that mentors require support and development, not least because good teachers are not automatically good mentors. However, there is little systematic training offered and few materials available to support mentors. Derrick and Dicks (2005) maintain that mentoring must become integral to the work of all experienced teachers to improve the quality of teacher training. It should be recognised as a formal aspect of their duties and rewarded by recognition, status, remission and remuneration.

## Funding

Current approaches to initial teacher training are inconsistent, with a plethora of programmes offering different organisational models, costs and fees (Casey, 2005). Training is offered in both higher and further education but with different funding and fees. These differential funding and fee structures are viewed as deeply problematic since they have produced severe inequities in funding that have led to disparities and discrepancies in the fees charged for training places (Casey, 2005; Lucas *et al.*, 2004; Ofsted, 2005). University courses are funded through the Higher Education Funding Council for England (HEFCE), whereas further education programmes are funded through the Learning and Skills Council at levels that do not return the full costs of providing quality teacher training. One reason is that delivering the subject knowledge specification as well as the PGCE or Cert. Ed makes these courses more expensive to provide than generic courses (Lucas *et al.*, 2005). This has implications for both the viability of courses and the higher fees that participants might be asked to pay. This could function as an additional deterrent to self-funded new entrants and place large financial burdens on learning providers who fund their staff to train.

### In-service training

The literature indicates that effective ESOL teaching is a complex process. Teacher expertise is a complex mix of values, beliefs, understanding of conceptual and theoretical frameworks, and ability to use a range of appropriate pedagogies. Continuing development therefore is likely to be most effective when it provide spaces for critical reflection and opportunities for teachers to develop their teacher identity, vision, skills and practices within the frameworks of the wider communities of practice.

Morton *et al.* (2006) stress that training and professional development should continue throughout a teacher's career. Access to relevant continuing professional development is critical to support them to develop and update their understanding, knowledge and pedagogic practices. This will help ensure that they bring informed and creative approaches to teaching. Baynham *et al.* (2007) conclude that developing teacher's 'professional vision' and encouraging 'an interpretive and reflective stance on teaching and learning' should be critical elements of continuing professional development. Similarly Morton *et al.* (2006) recommend that training should encourage teachers to explore their beliefs and values about teaching, but stress that this should be underpinned by a process of critical reflection within the context of explicit conceptual frameworks.

ESOL teachers tend to be enthusiastic and hungry for continuing professional development (Dalziel and Sofres, 2005b). However, anecdotal evidence to the NIACE ESOL inquiry (NIACE, 2006) suggests that the offer is not systematic and differs between areas. This echoes the findings of a recent survey of professional development in further education that also found a lack of cohesion and coherence in the provision of professional development as well as no clear teachers' entitlement and a shortage of funding (LLUK, 2006).

Formal training is only one aspect of continuing professional development. Opportunities for peers to learn informally and share expertise through practitioner networks can provide very fertile sources of professional development and mutual support (Barton and Papen, 2005; Sunderland, 2006). Training and development alongside colleagues from other organisations stimulates practice and helps to keep provision dynamic. It also boosts the teachers who suffer from professional isolation because they are the sole ESOL teacher, work in a very small team or work part-time (Dalziel and Sofres, 2005a). This is particularly likely in some workplaces, community organisations or prisons offering a small amount of ESOL. These communities of practice also provide mechanisms for linking research to practice and supporting practitioners to carry out research (Hillier and Thompson, 2005).

Participation in practitioner research is an empowering and motivating form of professional development. It offers opportunities to step back from day to day teaching to take a fresh look at practice (Hamilton *et al.*, 2007). As teachers investigate and reflect on their own practice, their knowledge and understanding deepens and practice changes, often becoming more enriched, exciting and effective (Hamilton, 2006a; Ivanič and Tseng, 2005; Ward with Edwards, 2002). However, opportunities for practitioner research are not widespread and, as Ward with Edwards (2002) found, recognition of the value of this activity is far from universal within the further education sector. Moreover, it can be difficult to source funding for this type of activity as research can be seen as a luxury in target-driven organisational cultures.

## Training for other staff

Quality ESOL provision depends not just on teachers, but on all staff associated with the learners. These include subject teachers, managers, outreach staff, and workers in the many agencies supporting adult speakers of other languages such as asylum seeker and refugee or migrant worker support organisations, homeless people's shelters or health workers. The training developed for adult literacy or specialist subject teachers will not necessarily meet their needs to know to how to advise on language or contribute to language skills development as an integral aspect of their primary work. The value of embedded ESOL approaches has been discussed. Extending and strengthening this type of provision will require subject teachers to be trained, but it is not yet clear how they will acquire the pedagogical knowledge they need in the context of the reformed teacher training frameworks.

Cultural and linguistic awareness training assists frontline staff to understand the needs of ESOL learners, cultural differences and expectations, and strategies for effective communication between people who speak different languages (Ward, 2004). The strength of community outreach workers lies in their knowledge of the communities in which they are located, their ability to communicate and recruit and encourage new learners because of their status and position of trust in the community, and their ability to empathise with and support learners. Employability frequently depends on gaining formal qualifications to complement this community knowledge understanding and skills. However, the current standards and qualifications do not reflect this skill set, thus are not necessarily the most appropriate for workers undertaking these types of activities (Dalziel and Sofres, 2005b).

The message from Ofsted (2005) is that leadership, management and quality assurance of ESOL is 'often weak' in GFE colleges. It is strong where managers at all levels of an organisation understand what ESOL is. This entails awareness of matters such as the relationship between ESOL and EFL, literacy, and other curriculum areas, the national ESOL infrastructure, ESOL theoretical concepts, pedagogical practice, quality debates and the qualities, training and support that ESOL teachers require. It appears that this is frequently not the case and development in this area could do a great deal to ensure that all ESOL learners can access high-quality, appropriate English language provision.

# 7 Funding

ESOL is currently funded from a range of sources through a number of different streams, each governed by different eligibility rules, targets and reporting requirements. This complexity has created much confusion for learners, learning organisations and advisors. Skills for Life is a priority within the planning and funding allocations of the Learning and Skills Council which funds most ESOL provision. Significant budgets have been allocated to ESOL Massive increases in demand and expenditure, along with shifts in government priorities and targets mean that the question of funding has become increasingly pertinent. The LSC started to question whether some learners and employers should be required to pay, and commissioned a review of ESOL funding which reported in 2005 (KPMG, 2005; LSC, 2004). In the Autumn of 2006 the LSC announced that the current entitlement of all settled immigrants, EU citizens, refugees, asylum seekers to free ESOL will cease from September 2007 when fees will be introduced (LSC, 2006b). This chapter sets out the current funding framework, and identifies the challenges and the questions related to funding ESOL.

## Learning and Skills Council funding for ESOL

As described earlier, there has been a huge increase in demand for ESOL, particularly in London where approximately half of all ESOL learners and expenditure are located. Nationally, ESOL enrolments on Learning and Skills Council funded provision rose from 159,000 in 2001/2 to an estimated 504,000 in 2005/6 (DfES, 2007). In the same period, spending rose from £103 million in 2001–02 to approximatley £270 million in 2005–06, just under 14 per cent of the adult learning budget for that year. A further increase to around £323 milion is predicted for 2007–08. Notwithstanding this increase in funding, current allocations are insufficient to provide free provision for all who wish to develop their English language skills. There are lengthy waiting lists in London and other urban conurbations, some rural areas are experiencing unprecedented demand and providers predict further growth. There are also localities, usually rural, where there is little demand for ESOL and this deters providers from offering dedicated ESOL classes as it is difficult or impossible to cover the costs of small classes under the present funding arrangements (Atkin *et al.*, 2005).

The LSC has reviewed who and what ESOL funding is to pay for (KPMG, 2005). At issue is what is to be expected of the state, individuals and employers. One view is that there is no inherent rationale for a welfare model, especially when some people are willing and able to fund their learning or have employers who will pay (LSC, 2006a). However, the concept of ability to pay opens the way towards a two-tier service which privileges those who can afford fees. The notion of affordability is complex, especially when it concerns low-paid workers, including those who support families overseas. Some long-term settled and recently-arrived migrant workers in well-paid employment might well consider that paying for training to enhance their earnings and employment prospects is a worthwhile investment and have the resources to pay (LSC, 2006b). Many others will not be a position to do so. In evidence to the NIACE ESOL inquiry (NIACE, 2006) learners indicated that they would be prepared to pay if they could, but said that finding the money to pay fees would be impossible. It will be important not to return to a division of provision founded on ability to pay rather than learning needs.

International comparisons indicate diverse approaches to language learning entitlements for migrants (Dutton, 2006). Refugees and asylum seekers are rarely in a position to pay for learning, and other countries have adopted policies that prioritise refugees and asylum seekers for free provision (Dutton, 2006; KPMG, 2005). Many countries, recognising the importance of language for all migrants offer entitlement to tuition, often linked to an explicit purpose, for instance integration in Denmark and Germany and professional and social independence in the Netherlands. Tuition is often free although it can be limited to a specific number of years or hours of learning; at the time of writing three years in Canada and Denmark and 600 hours in the Netherlands.

## Funding changes

The LSC announced in its annual statement of priorities (LSC, 2006b) that from September 2007 all ESOL learners will have to pay fees unless they are in receipt of means-tested benefits, and that asylum seekers over the age of 19 would no longer be eligible to access publicly-funded learning provision on arrival in England. This was met with dismay and criticism and prompted a save ESOL campaign spearheaded by the University and College Union (UCU).[3]

The DfES subsequently carried out a Race Equality Impact Assessment (DfES, 2007) where a number of important concerns were expressed. It is imperative that people from the settled migrant community and refugees and asylum seekers who are not able to pay are not disadvantaged, but there is widespread alarm that new proposals will have just this effect. Those who subsist on very low incomes, especially refugees and women with no independent income are particularly vulnerable to exclusion. Respondents feared that the proposals will further exclude under-represented women who either do not have access to independent or family income or cannot obtain evidence of entitlement to fee remission because of family attitudes to their learning. A further group in danger of exclusion through the new proposals are low-paid workers who cannot afford to pay fees and whose employers will not pay.

There was disquiet about the disparity between ESOL and literacy as it appears inequitable to be charging one group of learners and creating a divide that some regard as racist. There is also alarm about proposals to remove entitlement from adult asylum seekers, with opponents pointing out that denying access to language learning is harsh and unjust, will almost certainly cause a great deal of hardship for individuals and has negative implications for community cohesion.

The government introduced a number of measures designed to address the concerns raised in the Race Equality Impact Assessment. These include reinstatement of eligibility for asylum seekers who have not received a decision on their application after six months, or who are unable to leave for reasons beyond their control. Vulnerable learners, including spouses and low-paid workers will be able to

3 See http://www.ucu.org.uk/index.cfm

access support through a Hardship fund which will be introduced for 2007/8.

### Employers' contributions

There is a government expectation that employers and employment agencies should invest in training for developing their workforces, especially when they recruit from overseas. The ESOL Pathfinder projects found that while employers regarded as having poor employment practices were reluctant to pay staff for training, others readily appreciated the benefits of ESOL and were successfully persuaded to contribute to the costs of training their workforce (Dalziel and Sofres, 2005b). However, the current system for employer engagement in workforce development is based on voluntarism and, while employers are encouraged to develop learning opportunities for their workforces through the new 'Employer Pledge', there is no element of compulsion to do so, at least in the short term, or sanctions for failing to offer or fund development opportunities. The varying spectrum of employment practices for migrant workers highlighted in earlier chapters indicates that it is fairly certain that there will be no across the board employer and agency agreement to invest in workforce language development. Could we imagine the Morecambe Bay cockle pickers' gang masters investing in language classes for instance? On the other hand, some employers can be persuaded of the economic returns of investing in training. More work is required to investigate how bringing about greater employer investment in ESOL could best be managed.

## What ESOL is funded?

Current criteria for *Skills for Life* funding are that provision must be based on the national standards for adult literacy and numeracy, and meet the needs of learners from entry level up to and including level 2. ESOL has been free for eligible learners and the Learning and Skills Council pays 100 per cent of the national funding rate. In addition, all eligible learners attract a disadvantage uplift of 12 per cent, and ESOL learning aims are weighted at 1.4 (LSC, 2006a). This means that ESOL is relatively generously funded in acknowledgement of the additional costs entailed in providing necessary levels of support and staff-learner ratios. In return, the LSC expects learning organisations to supply high-quality ESOL free to eligible learners. One group who have been consistently excluded are newly-arrived spouses and family members of permanent UK residents; a group which is predominantly women. As noted in Chapter 2, they are not eligible for state-funded provision for at least one year after arrival with negative consequences for their prospects and settlement, but the new funding regime has failed to address this inequity.

The Skills strategy (DfES 2005f) determines funding priorities. This has profound consequences for what provision, and therefore which learners, get funded and for what purposes. Evidence to the NIACE ESOL inquiry (NIACE, 2006) revealed deep disquiet about the ways in which the tight link between funding and national targets appears to be leading to rigid approaches to funding that mean provision is not tuned to the needs of all learners, especially older learners who are not aiming to enter the workforce, learners at entry level and adults who want short work-focused courses. Evans *et al.* (2006), for instance, find that funding is not sufficiently flexible for migrant workers who need language training that fits with their employment patterns.

Others worry that funding is being directed towards level 1 and 2 accredited provision to the disadvantage of learners at entry level. Since January 2005 only nationally-approved ESOL qualifications have been eligible for *Skills for Life* funding. The Learning and Skills Council aims for providers to shift the majority of their provision to programmes offering these qualifications and has introduced a benchmark of an 80/20 percentage split between learners working towards nationally-approved qualifications and those not (LSC, 2006a). It is unclear what evidence has informed the decision to split the provision 80/20 and to what extent this reflects learners' priorities.

National guidance (LSC, 2006a) makes it clear that the 20 per cent is provision for learners not enrolled on a nationally-approved qualification, including those at pre-entry level, and the 80 per cent includes nationally-approved qualifications at Entry Levels 1, 2 and 3 and Levels 1 and 2. Despite this, evidence submitted to the NIACE ESOL inquiry (NIACE, 2006) indicates that local funding allocations have started to prioritise funding for Level 1 and 2 provision. This is to support achievement of the LSC Public Service Agreement (PSA) targets which are expressed as achievements of nationally-approved qualifications at Entry Level 3 and Levels 1 and 2.

The problem with this manipulation of provision to fit funding streams and meet targets is that it might not reflect learners' actual levels and needs. Reducing providers' ability to satisfy the demand from learners at entry level is particularly worrying because rationing provision can be jeopardising their futures. Where this happens learners' futures can be jeopardised because shrinking entry provision disrupts progression ladders into the higher levels needed for access to vocational provision and securing employment. Bynner and Parsons (2006) have drawn on data from longitudinal cohort studies to demonstrate a close correlation between reduced life chances, social exclusion, poor access to the labour market and literacy and numeracy skills at or below Entry Level 2. If this holds true for English language skills, these findings imply that it is imperative to enhance rather than reduce provision that enables adults to reach and progress beyond these levels. It is therefore not certain that the current balance will secure the progression routes required to meet the economic priorities of current policy (DfES, 2005f), and even less that it will advance social inclusion and settlement.

The narrowing of priorities also affects the life chances of refugees and asylum seekers who require higher-level qualifications for entry to employment and higher-level study. IELTS qualifications are a requirement for overseas medical professionals wishing to practice in the UK. However as these qualifications are ineligible for LSC *Skills for Life* funding, learners must pay fees unless alternative funding can be sourced. While charges for provision leading to a well-paid career might be entirely reasonable for some groups of bilingual adults, they also close the door to many refugees and asylum seekers with professional backgrounds aspiring to gain employment in their previous profession.

Reduced funding is detrimental to other areas of work that fall outside ESOL classroom delivery. Crèches enable parents, usually women to attend, and many are excluded as there are insufficient places. Embedded learning approaches are expensive as they incur additional costs to support ESOL and vocational staff to adopt colla-borative approaches to developing, planning and teaching; these are not sufficiently recognised in current funding arrangements (Dalziel and Sofres, 2005a; Eldred, 2005; Roberts *et al.*, 2005). The adults who do not readily come forward for places, again usually women, as discussed in Chapter 3, need additional interventions and often find the prospect of attending classes in venues close to home more attractive. However, dispersed provision is more expensive to run and this can deter some organisations from offering it.

Similarly, many of the initiatives and approaches that widen participation and improve quality are expensive, and it is difficult to draw down core funding for development and outreach work. Resources for innovation are often time-limited and tied to targets that are externally imposed rather than negotiated at grass roots level. Yet, this is the work that is needed to draw in the excluded learners whose needs are overshadowed by those more confident to demand places. Establishing and maintaining relationships with partner organisations, including employers and community groups, requires a significant investment in time and energy. This is essential for underpinning developments in workplace ESOL and the contribution of community organisation to recruiting, advising and supporting learners, but funding for this area of work is often difficult to identify.

The new funding arrangements have not taken effect at the time of writing so it is not yet possible to comment on their impact. Undoubtedly the issue of financing ESOL, to bring about access for all, needs to be addressed. However, unless it is carried out within the spirit of policy commitments to inclusion and equality, as well as to economic development and increasing prosperity, the people suffering highest levels of exclusion will be denied opportunities to develop the language skills they need to combat these disadvantages and take control over their lives. The current approach is not inevitable, and access to English is such a fundamental prerequisite for personal autonomy, choice, and economic and social justice that the alternative of increasing the level of ESOL funding should be seriously considered.

# 8 Conclusion

This overview of the contemporary context of ESOL reveals a cratered landscape pitted with many challenges. Many of these are not new but have been endemic for many years, while others are old issues resurfacing in a different form. What has changed are demographic factors, policy contexts and funding climates. ESOL is characterised by diversity and complexity, and current dialogues and dilemmas concern the most effective ways to respond. The most salient thematic features of ESOL emerging from the literature are summarised below.

## Learners

English language learners, always diverse have become even more so. There are commonalities within and across different groups of migrants, but also a huge amount of diversity in their life stories, cultural, educational and work histories and personal circumstances. The literature indicates that ESOL policy, organisation, teaching and funding has not been sufficiently tuned to respond to all learners' disparate needs which require multiple solutions. Consequently particular needs are not addressed and some groups and individuals are more likely to be either excluded from provision or not effectively supported to progress within it.

References to gender thread through the literature but, with a few exceptions, there is little specific focus or attention on this issue and nowhere are the strands drawn together. Women's migration experiences, life circumstances, work histories, and employment patterns are different from those of men. Their rates of participation in the labour market and employment potential are often overlooked. They are more likely to experience harassment and abuse, and lack of independence or other gender-related cultural factors can restrict opportunities to take up learning.

## Purpose of ESOL

ESOL is usually presented in terms of advancing economic prosperity and bringing about greater social inclusion and community cohesion. The literature points to imbalances in the weight accorded to each, with language for skills and employment seen to be in ascendancy.

Perceptions of the purpose of ESOL range along a spectrum where equipping learners to operate in society as it is sits at one end, and the more transformative position of ESOL as a mechanism for supporting adults to change social, political and economic conditions at the other.

The research suggests that ESOL learners are more likely to live in disadvantaged circumstances in marginalised communities and encounter social injustice, discrimination, or racism. ESOL can offer a potent tool to combat these inequalities, especially when underpinned by anti-racist perspectives, although it is acknowledged it will not work unless situated in a context of other integrated social and economic interventions.

The literature illustrates the way in which ESOL is treated in isolation through education policy and funding although the evidence indicates that multi-agency, cross-policy approaches best address social justice, settlement and integration.

## ESOL teaching and learning

The question of what processes provide the most effective means of working with learners to support them to achieve their aims is highly contested territory. Views are extremely polarised and more research and development is needed to find solutions to the challenges of how best to identify and respond to individual needs in group learning environments in ways that support learning and achievement and foster empowerment, choice and autonomy.

Studies conclude that as language learning is such a complex process there is no one 'right' teaching approach that will suit all learners or guarantee progress. A balance and variety of activities is more likely to be effective.

Experienced teachers develop 'professional knowledge' that provides them with a frame of reference that enables them to engage in critical reflection, operate responsively in classroom situations as well as to critique and make sense of the demands arising from the wider policy context and translate these into effective classroom practice.

The social practice perspectives illuminated in the research provide a powerful argument that language development is richer and more effective when it takes into account both linguistic items and the cultural, economic, social and political contexts and power structures within which language transactions and interactions take place. It follows from this that ESOL will be more effective when related to the real-life contexts in which language will be used.

## The ESOL workforce

It is widely recognised that the expertise of ESOL teachers is a major factor in successful language development. However, recruiting and training sufficient numbers of ESOL teachers poses huge challenges. Pay and conditions act as a deterrent to recruitment. Routes into the profession are poorly developed and training structures are in a state of flux as reforms of post-16 learning and *Skills for Life* are introduced.

The challenges of developing teacher education to meet the diverse training needs of new entrants and established teachers have not been fully resolved. Teacher education structures are being reformed and reshaped and it is imperative that the new frameworks take account of the challenges posed in training ESOL teachers who need to get to grips with both subject knowledge and language teaching practices.

## Funding

Funding for learners is a contentious and problematic area. Put simply, the problem is that there is more demand than funding allocated for provision to meet it and a rationing, fee-based approach has been introduced as a result.

This has been met with widespread disquiet and opposition to the measures is focused on the fear that the most disadvantaged adults will be excluded from ESOL.

## Research

The research base for ESOL is developing but still relatively thin. Drawing on research can help us find creative solutions to resolve many of the challenges outlined above. Although we can find some answers in current practice and expertise in the field, we urgently need to expand our knowledge to answer questions concerning the most effective ESOL models and pedagogic practices.

Early priorities for the research agenda might include pedagogic practice, especially bilingual and embedded approaches, addressing individual needs in group learning contexts, effective ways of using ICT and ESOL literacy, gender and the cross-cultural and linguistic factors that impact on meeting the needs of learners with disabilities and learning difficulties. We also need to discover more systematic ways of using research findings to inform policy making and practice.

## The future

The shifts in learner populations and demand require radical solutions. Reformist tinkering round the edges of ESOL is unlikely to result in the fundamental changes needed to benefit learners and enable teachers to concentrate on delivering effective language learning to empower learners to achieve their goals and aspirations and develop as independent, reflective learners. We need critical reflection on ways in which the world has changed in order to take a fresh look at what we want to take forward, start anew or drop.

Perhaps the questions to ask concern how to develop English language skills in ways that liberate learners to gain more independence and control over their lives. ESOL was originally developed to address poverty and support the inclusion of recently-arrived immigrants. Rediscovering ways of linking language learning to the social contexts of exclusion and disadvantage would direct resources for ESOL to combat racism, poverty and exclusion and contribute to a more equitable and just society in which migrants are valued and enabled to thrive.

# References

Adult Learning Inspectorate (2003) *Annual Report of the Chief Inspector 2002–03*. London: ALI.

Adult Learning Inspectorate (2004a) *Annual Report of the Chief Inspector 2003–04*. London: ALI.

Adult Learning Inspectorate (2004b) *Basic Skills for offenders in the community*. London: ALI.

Adult Learning Inspectorate (2005) *Annual Report of the Chief Inspector 2004–05*. London: ALI.

ALBSU (1989) *A Nation's neglect*. London: Adult Literacy and Basic Skills Unit.

ALBSU (1992) 'ESOL – Time to start afresh?' *Newsletter*, Spring No. 45. London: Adult Literacy and Basic Skills Unit.

ALBSU (1993a) *Parents and Their Children: the intergenerational effects of poor basic skills*. London: Adult Literacy and Basic Skills Unit.

ALBSU (1993b) *The Cost to Industry: basic skills and the UK workforce*. London: Adult Literacy and Basic Skills Unit.

ALI/Ofsted (2001) *The Common Inspection framework for inspecting post-16 Education and training*. London: Adult Learning Inspectorate, Ofsted.

Aldridge, F., Dutton, Y., Gray, R., McLoughlin, A., Sterland, L. and Waddington, S. (2005) *Working to Rebuild Careers*. Leicester: NIACE.

Aldridge, F. and Tuckett, A. (2003) *Light and Shade*. Leicester: NIACE.

Aldridge, F. and Waddington, S. (2002) *Asylum Seekers' Skills and Qualifications Audit Pilot Project*. Leicester: NIACE.

Ananiadou, K., Jenkins, A. and Wolf, A. (2003) *The Benefits to Employers of Raising Workforce Basic Skills Levels: a review of the literature*. London: National Research and Development Centre for Adult Literacy and Numeracy.

Archer (2005) in Barton, D. and Papen, U. (eds.) *Linking literacy and numeracy programmes in developing countries and the UK*. Lancaster: NRDC.

Armstrong, D. and Heathcote V. (2003) *Literature Review of ESOL for learners with learning difficulties and/or disabilities.* London: NRDC.

Atkin, C., Rose, A. and Shier, R. (2005) *Provision of, and learner engagement with, adult literacy, numeracy and ESOL support in rural England.* London: NRDC.

Audit Commission (2007) *Crossing Borders. Responding to the challenges of migrant workers for local authorities.* London: Audit Commission.

Barton, D. and Papen, U. (2005) *Linking literacy and numeracy programmes in developing countries and the UK.* Lancaster London: NRDC.

Barton, D. and Pitt, K. (2003) *Adult ESOL pedagogy: a review of research, an annotated bibliography and recommendations for future research.* London: NRDC.

Basic Skills Agency (2001) *The National Basic Skills Strategy for Wales.* London: Basic Skills Agency/ National Assembly for Wales, http://www.basic-skills-wales.org/bsastrategy/resources/Welsh%20Strategy%202001%20(English).pdf

Baynham, M., Roberts, C., Cooke, M., Simpson, J. and Ananiadou, K. Callaghan, J., McGoldrick, J. and Wallace, C. (2007) *Effective teaching and learning ESOL.* London: NRDC.

Berkeley, R., Khan, O. and Ambikaipaker, M. (2006) *What's new about new immigrants in twenty-first century Britain?* Joseph Rowntree Foundation http://www.jrf.org.uk/bookshop/eBooks/9781899354440.pdf

Blackledge A. (2006) *Literacy, Power and Social Justice.* Stoke on Trent: Trentham.

Bloch, A. (2002) *Refugees' opportunities and barriers in employment and training.* DWP Research report 179.

Bloch, A. (2004) 'Labour Market Participation and Conditions of Employment: A Comparison of Minority Ethnic Groups and Refugees in Britain'. *Sociological Research Online*, Vol. 9, No.2. http://www.socresonline.org.uk/9/2/bloch.html

Bradford Central and Eastern European Working Group (2006) *A8 Migration in Bradford. A Template for action.* Bradford.

Braggins, J. and Talbot, J. (2003) *Time to Learn. Prisoners' views on prison education.* London: Prison Reform Trust.

Bray, K. (2004) *Our Rights, Our Choice.* Disability Rights Commission, www.drc.org.uk

Breen, M. (2001) 'The social context for language learning: a neglected situation?' in Candlin C. and Mercer N. (eds.) *English language teaching in its social context: A reader.* London: Routledge.

Brooks, G., Harman, J., Hutchison, D., Kendall, S. and Wilkin, A. (1999). *Family Literacy for New Groups: The National Foundation for Educational Research Evaluation of the Basic Skills Agency's Programmes for Linguistic Minorities, Year 4 and Year 7*. London: Basic Skills Agency.

Brooks, G., Giles, K., Harman, J., Kendall, S., Rees, F. and Whittaker, S. (2001) *Assembling the Fragments: a review of research on adult basic skills*. London: Department for Education and Employment.

Bynner, J. and Parsons, S. (1997) *It Doesn't Get any Better*. London: Basic Skills Agency.

Bynner, J. and Parsons, S. (2006) *New Light on Literacy and Numeracy*. London: NRDC.

CAB (2004) *Nowhere to turn – CAB evidence on the exploitation of migrant workers* http://www.citizensadvice.org.uk/nowhere-to-turn.pdf accessed 2.2.06.

Callaghan, J. (2004) 'Diversity, ILPs, and the art of the possible,' *Reflect*, Vol. 1, pp. 6–7.

Carneiro, P., Meghir, C. Parey, M. (2006) *Intergenerational effects of mother's schooling on children's outcomes: causal links and transmission channels*. London: UCL.

Carr-Hill R., Passingham S., Wolf A., Kent N. (1996) *Lost Opportunities: the language skills of linguistic minorities in England and Wales*. London: Basic Skills Agency.

Casey, H. (2005) 'Skills for Life and teacher education: the continuing challenges'. *Reflect*, Vol. 4, pp. 4–6.

Casey, H., Cara, O., Eldred, J., Grief, S., Hodge, R., Ivanič, R., Jupp, T., Lopez, D. and McNeil, B. (2006) *'You wouldn't expect a maths teacher to teach plastering…' Embedding literacy, language and numeracy in post-16 vocational programmes – the impact on learning and achievement*. London: NRDC.

Clarke, A. (2005) 'Personal reflections on training teachers to use ICT', *Reflect*, Vol. 4, pp. 11.

Clarke, A. and Englebright, L. (2003) *ICT The New Basic Skill*. Leicester: NIACE.

Colville, R. (2006) 'The Perfect Scapegoat'. *Refugees*, Vol. 1, No. 142, pp. 7–19.

Commission on Integration and Cohesion (2006) *Our Interim report*, London: Commission on Integration and Cohesion.

Commission on Integration and Cohesion (2007) *Our Shared Future*, London: Commission on Integration and Cohesion.

Condelli, L. (2002) *Effective Instruction for Adult ESL Literacy Learners: Findings from the 'What work' study*. Washington DC: American Institutes for Research.

Connexions (2003) *Working Together, Supporting Young Asylum Seekers and Refugees,* Sheffield: Department for Education and Skills http://www.renewal.net/Documents/RNET/Policy%20Guidance/Workingtogetherconnexions.pdf

Cooke, M., Wallace, C. with Shrubshall, P. (2004) in Roberts, C., Baynham, M., Shrubshall, P., Barton, D., Chopra, P., Cooke, M., Hodge, R., Pitt, K., Schellekens, P., Wallace, C. and Whitfield, S. *English for Speakers of Other Languages (ESOL) – case studies of provision, learners' needs and resources.* London: NRDC.

Crick, B. (2006) 'Language Games'. *Prospect*, July, p. 16.

Crowther, J., Hamilton, M. and Tett, L. (2001) *Powerful Literacies*. Leicester: NIACE.

Dalziel, D. and Sofres T.N. (2005a) *ESOL Pathfinder Learners' Survey and Prisons Report*. London: DFES.

Dalziel, D. and Sofres T. N. (2005b) *Qualitative Evaluation of the ESOL* Pathfinder Projects. London, DFES.

DCLG (2006) *Strong and prosperous communities*. London: Department for Communities and Local Government.

Derrick, J. and Dicks, J. (2005) *Teaching practice and mentoring*. Leicester: NIACE.

DfEE (1998) *The Learning Age*. London: Department for Education and Employment.

DfEE (1999) *A Fresh Start: improving literacy and numeracy*. London: Department for Education and Employment.

DfEE (2000) *Breaking the Language Barriers: The report of the working group on English for speakers of other languages*. London: Department for Education and Employment.

DfEE (2001a) *Skills for Life: the national strategy for improving adult literacy and numeracy*. London: Department for Education and Employment.

DfES (2001b) *Adult ESOL core curriculum*. London: Department for Education and Skills.

DfES (2002) *Success for All*. London: Department for Education and Skills.

DfES (2003a) *Planning learning and recording progress and achievement*. London: Department for Education and Skills.

DfES (2003b) *Skills for Life, the national strategy for improving adult literacy and numeracy skills. Focus on delivery to 2007*. London: Department for Education and Skills.

DfES (2003c) *21st Century skills: 'Realising our Potential'*. London: Department for Education and Skills.

DfES (2004a) *Equipping our Teachers for the Future: Reforming Initial Teacher Training for the Learning and Skills Sector*. London: Department for Education and Skills.

DfES (2004b) *ESOL Pathfinder. Working with employers*. London: Department for Education and Skills.

DfES (2005a) *Case Studies ESOL and ICT*. London: Department for Education and Skills.

DfES (2005b) *Extended schools: Access to services and opportunities for all. A prospectus*. London: Department for Education and Skills.

DfES (2005c) *Reducing reoffending though skills and employment*. London: Department for Education and Skills.

DfES (2005d) *Skills for Families*. London: Department for Education and Skills.

DfES (2005e) *Skills for Communities*. London: Department for Education and Skills.

DfES (2005f) *Skills: Getting on in business, getting on at work*. London: Department for Education and Skills.

DfES (2006a) *ESOL Access for All, Guidance on making the adult ESOL curriculum accessible Part 1*. London: Department for Education and Skills.

DfES (2006b) *ESOL Access for All, Guidance on making the adult ESOL curriculum accessible Part 2*. London: Department for Education and Skills.

DfES (2006c) *It's not as simple as you think. Cultural viewpoints around disability*. London: Department for Education and Skills.

DfES (2006d) *Making it happen: An inclusive approach to working with people with learning difficulties who have ESOL needs*. London: Department for Education and Skills.

DfES (2007) *Race Equality impact assessment on proposed changes to the funding arrangements for English for Speakers of Other Languages and asylum seeker eligibility for Learning and Skills Council Further education funding – report and emerging proposals*.
http://www.dfes.gov.uk/readwriteplus/bank/ACF1BE9.pdf

DfES/FENTO (2002) *Subject Specifications for teachers of English for Speakers of Other Languages (ESOL)*. London: Department for Education and Skills.

DWP (2005) *Working to Rebuild Lives. A Refugee Employment Strategy*. London: Department of Work and Pensions.

DWP (2006) *A new deal for welfare: Empowering people to work*. London: Department of Work and Pensions.

Dumper, H. (2002) *Is it safe here? Refugee women's experiences in the UK*. London: Refugee Action.

Dustmann, C. and Fabbri, F. (2003) 'Language Proficiency and Labour Market Performance of Immigrants in the UK'. *The Economic Journal*, Vol. 113, pp. 695–717.

Dutton, N., Eldred, J., Ward, J. (2005) *Catching Confidence*. Leicester: NIACE.

Dutton, N. (2006) Comparison of approaches to language learning for migrants in different countries, unpublished paper written for the NIACE ESOL committee of Inquiry.

Eldred, J. (2005) *Developing embedded literacy, language and numeracy: supporting achievement*. Leicester: NIACE.

Employability Forum (2004) *Silver Lining. Integrating refugee skills into the workforce – a strategy for refugee nurses*. London: Employability Forum.

Erel, U. and Tomlinson, F. (2005) *Women refugees – from volunteers to employees: a research project on paid and unpaid work in the voluntary sector and volunteering as a pathway into employment*. London: Working Lives Research Institute http://www.workinglives.org/volunteers.html.

Evans, C., Pye, J. and Smith, L. (2006) *Migrant Workers: The Challenge for the South West*. Exeter: Marchmont Observatory.

FENTO (2002) *Guidance on using the Subject Specifications for teachers of English for Speakers of other languages (ESOL) at level 4 in conjunction with the Standards for teaching and supporting learning*. London: FENTO.

Freire, P. (1972) *Pedagogy of the Oppressed*. Middlesex: Penguin.

Gilpin, N., Henty, M., Lemos, S., Portes, J. and Bullen, C. (2006) *The impact of free movement of workers from Central and Eastern Europe on the UK labour market*. Working Paper No. 29. London: Department for Work and Pensions http://www.dwp.gov.uk/asd/asd5/wp29.pdf

Greenslade, R. (2005) *Seeking Scapegoats. The coverage of asylum in the UK press*. London: Institute for Public Policy Research.

Gregory, E. (1996) 'Learning from the Community: A family literacy project with Bangladeshi-origin children in London', in Wolfendale, S. and Topping, K. (eds.) *Family Involvement in Literacy*. London: Cassell.

Grief, S. and Taylor, C. (2002) *Evaluation of the Basic Skills and ESOL in Local Communities Projects*. Coventry: LSC.

Grief, S. and Windsor, V. (2002) *Recognising and Validating Learning Outcomes and Achievements in Non-accredited Basic Skills and ESOL.* London: Learning and Skills Development Agency.

Hamilton, M. (2006a) 'Practitioner research. Just a fling...or a long-term relationship?' *Reflect*, No. 6, pp. 14–16.

Hamilton, M. (2006b) *Putting Words in their Mouths: The Alignment of Identities with System Goals through the use of Individual Learning Plans*, Lancaster http://www.literacy.lancs.ac.uk/what/Mary-Hamilton-papers.pdf

Hamilton, M. and Barton, D. (2000) 'The International Literacy survey: what does it measure?' *International review of education*, Vol. 46 No. 5.

Hamilton, M and Hillier, Y. (2006) *Changing Faces*. Stoke on Trent: Trentham Books.

Hamilton, M. and Merrifield, J. (2000) 'Adult learning and literacy in the United Kingdom', in Comings J., Garner, B. and Smith, C. (eds.) *Annual Review of Adult Learning and Literacy volume 1*. San Francisco: Jossey-Bass.

Hamilton, M., Davies, P. and James, K. (2007) (eds.) *Practitioners leading research*. London: NRDC.

Heath, A. and Cheung S. Y. (2006) *Ethnic penalties in the labour market: Employers and discrimination*. London: Department for Work and Pensions.

Hillage, J., Loukas, G., Newton, B. (2005) *Platform for Progression: Employer Training Pilots: Year 2 Evaluation Report.* www.dfes.gov.uk/research/data/uploadfiles/ETP2.pdf accessed February 2006.

Hillier, Y. and Thompson, A. (2005) *Readings in post-compulsory education. Research in the learning and skills sector*. London: Continuum.

Hodge, R. and Pitt, K. with Barton, D. (2004) *"This is not enough for one's life": Perceptions of living and learning English in Blackburn by learners seeking asylum and refugee status*. Lancaster; Lancaster University.

HM Government (2004) *Every Child Matters: Change for Children* http://www.everychildmatters.gov.uk

HM Government (2006) *Reaching out: An action plan on social exclusion.* London: Cabinet Office.

Home Office (2001) *Community Cohesion: a report of the independent review team chaired by Ted Cantle*. London: Home Office.

Home Office (2003) *The New and the Old. The report of the 'Life in the United Kingdom' Advisory Group*. London: Home Office Social Policy Unit.

Home Office (2004) *Skills Audit of Refugees*; online report 37/04. London: Home Office.

Home Office (2005a) *Improving Opportunity, Strengthening Society: The government's strategy to increase race equality and community cohesion*. London: Home Office.

Home Office (2005b) *Integration matters: A National Strategy for Refugee Integration*. London: Home Office.

Home Office, DWP, HM Revenue and Customs, ODPM (2006) *Accession Monitoring Report* May 2004–June 2006 http://www.ind.homeoffice.gov.uk/6353/aboutus/Revised_data_MT.final.pdf

Hughes, N., Paton, A. and Schwab, I. (2005) 'Theory, practice and professionalism in teacher education', *Reflect*, Vol. 4. pp. 8–9.

Hunt J. (2005) 'E-learning, Skills for Life and teacher training', *Reflect*, Vol. 4, pp. 10–12.

Hurstfield, J., Pearson, R., Hooker, H., Ritchie, H., Sinclair, A. (2004) *Employing Refugees: Some Organisations' Experiences*, Brighton: Institute for Employment Studies http://www.employment-studies.co.uk/pdflibrary/ 01550ef.pdf accessed 4.02 06.

Ivanič, R. and Tseng, M. L. (2005) *Understanding the relationships between learning and teaching: an analysis of the contribution of applied linguistics*. London: NRDC.

Ivanič, R., Appleby, Y., Hodge, R., Tusting, K. and Barton, D. (2006) *Linking learning and everyday life: a social perspective on adult language, literacy and numeracy classes*. London: NRDC.

JH Consulting (2005) *Developing a Three Year Strategic Action Plan for Skills for Life in London. Summary of evidence and recommendations for ESOL*. London: LSC/LDA.

Julka, N. (2005) 'ILPs: related to real life?' *Reflect*, Vol. 2, pp. 31–32.

Kenner, C. (2007) Developing bilingual learning strategies in mainstream and community contexts, unpublished.

Kirk, R. (2004) *Skills Audit of refugees*, Home Office Online Report 37/04 http://www.homeoffice.gov.uk/rds/pdfs04/rdsolr3704.pdf

Kofman, E., Raghuram, P. and Merefield, M (2005) *Gendered Migrations: Towards gender sensitive policies in the UK*. London: Institute for Public Policy Research.

KPMG (2005) *KPMG Review of English for Speakers of Other Languages*. London: DfES/LSC.

Kyambi, S. (2005) *Beyond Black and White*. London: IPPR.

Lavender, P., Derrick J. and Brooks, B. (2004) *Testing, Testing...1 2 3' Assessment in adult Literacy, language and numeracy*. Leicester: NIACE.

Learning and Skills Council (2004) *Priorities for Success*. Coventry: LSC.

Learning and Skills Council (2006a) *Policy Requirements for Planning: Managing the Balance and Mix of Provision* (2006/07) http://www.lsc.gov.uk/National/Documents/SubjectListing/Funding Learning/managing_balance-mix-of-provision0607.htm accessed 10.02.06

Learning and Skills Council (2006b) *Raising our Game – Our Annual Statement of Priorities*. Coventry: LSC.

Leitch, S. (2005) *Skills in the UK: The long-term challenge* http://www.hm-treasury.gov.uk/independent_reviews/leitch_review/ review_leitch_index.cfm

Leitch, S. (2006) *Prosperity for all in the global economy – world class skills*. London: HM Treasury.

LLUK (2006) *Scoping of good practice in professional development among staff in further education and work based learning*. London: LLU.

Lopez, D. (2005) 'Reflect in Canada: using participatory methods in the ESOL classroom' in Barton, D. and Papen, U. (eds.) *Linking literacy and numeracy programmes in developing countries and the UK*. Lancaster, London: NRDC.

Lucas, N., Casey, H. and Giannakaki, M. (2004a) *Skills for Life core curriculum training programmes 2001/03: characteristics of teacher participants*. London: NRDC.

Lucas, N., Casey, H., Loo, S., McDonald, J. and Giannakaki, M. (2004b) *New initial teacher education programmes for teachers of literacy, numeracy and ESOL 2002/3: an exploratory study*. London: NRDC.

Lucas, N., Loo, S. and McDonald, J. (2005) 'Combining subject knowledge with how to teach: an exploratory study of new initial teacher education for teachers of adult literacy, numeracy and English for Speakers of Other Languages'. *International Journal of Lifelong Education*, Vol. 24, pp. 337–350.

Lyons, M. (2006) *National prosperity, local choice and civic engagement: a new partnership between central and local government for the 21st century,* http://www.lyonsinquiry.org.uk/docs/20060504%20Final%20Complete .pdf accessed August 8 2006

Lyons, M. (2007) *Place-shaping: a shared ambition for the future of local government.* London: The Stationery Office.

Mallows, D. (2006) *Insights: What research has to tell us about ESOL.* London: NRDC.

Maudsley, L., Rafique, A. and Uddin, A. (2003) *Aasha: working with young people with a learning difficulty from a South Asian background.* London: Skill.

McGoldrick, J., Turner, S. and Weinrich, F, with Cooke, M. (2007) 'ESOL and learner retention' in Hamilton, M., Davies, P. and James, K. (eds.) *Practitioners leading research.* London: NRDC.

Mellar, H., Kambouri, M., Sanderson, M. and Pavlou, V. (2004) *ICT and adult literacy, numeracy and ESOL.* London: NRDC.

Millman, L. (2005) 'English for Speakers of Caribbean Languages' in Barton, D. and Papen, U. (eds.) *Linking literacy and numeracy programmes in developing countries and the UK.* Lancaster, London: NRDC.

Morton, T., McGuire, T. and Baynham, M. (2006) *A literature review of research on teacher education in adult literacy, numeracy and ESOL.* London: NRDC.

Moss, M. and Southwood, S. (2006) *e-learning for teaching English for Speakers of Other Languages.* Leicester: NIACE.

National Statistics (2006) *Chinese pupils have the best GCSE results* http://www.statistics.gov.uk/cci/nugget.asp?id=461

NIACE and LLU+ (2005) *Citizenship materials for ESOL learners.* Leicester: NIACE.

NIACE (2006) *More than a language…,* Leicester: NIACE.

Norton, B. and Toohey, K. (2001) 'Changing perspectives on good language learners', *TESOL Quarterly,* Vol. 35 No. 2, pp. 307–22.

ODPM (2003) *Sustainable communities: building for the future.* London: Office of the Deputy Prime Minister.

ODPM (2004a) *Tackling Social exclusion: Taking stock and looking to the future.* London: Office of the Deputy Prime Minister.

ODPM (2004b) *The Egan review: skills for sustainable communities.* London: Office of the Deputy Prime Minister.

ODPM (2005) *Improving services, improving lives: evidence and key themes.* London: Office of the Deputy Prime Minister.

Office of National Statistics (2007) *Update on the Improving Migration and Population Statistics* (IMPS) Project – August 2006
http://www.statistics.gov.uk/about/data/methodology/specific/ population/future/imps/updates/downloads/Update_on_the_ Improving_Migration_and_Population_Statistics.pdf

Ofsted (2003) *The initial training of further education teachers*. London: Ofsted.

Ofsted (2005a) *Raising the achievement of bilingual learners*. London: Ofsted.

Ofsted (2005b) *Skills for life in colleges: one year on*. London: Ofsted.

Ofsted (2006) *The initial training of further education teachers. Findings from 2004/5 inspections of courses leading to national awarding body qualifications*. London: Ofsted.

Ofsted/ALI (2003) *Literacy, numeracy and English for speakers of other languages: a survey of current practice in post-16 and adult provision*. London: Ofsted.

Papen, U. (2005) *Adult Literacy as Social Practice*. London: Routledge.

Payne, J. (2003) *Basic Skills in the Workplace: a research review*. London: Learning and Skills Development Agency.

Phillimore, J., Craig L., Goodson, L. and Sankey, S. (2006) *Employability initiatives for refugees in Europe: looking at, and learning from, good practice*. Birmingham: Centre for Urban and Regional Studies.

Pitt, K. (2005) *Debates in ESOL Teaching and Learning*. London: Routledge.

Rees, S. and Sunderland, H (1990) *Not meeting the demand? A report into waiting lists, fees and provision in London*. London: Language and literacy Unit.

Rees, S. and Sunderland, H (1991) *Still not meeting the demand? A report of research into ESOL and language support waiting list and fees in FE and AEs*. London: Language and literacy Unit.

Rees, S., Savitzky, F. and Malik, A. (eds.) (2003) *On the Road. Journeys in family learning*. London: London Language and Literacy Unit.

Refugee Council (2002) *Credit to the Nation. Refugee contributions to the UK*. London: Refugee Council.

Refugee Council (2005a) *A study of asylum seekers with special needs*, http://www.refugeecouncil.org.uk/policy/position/2005/specialneeds. htm accessed 20.11.05

Refugee Council (2005b) *Making women visible*, http://www.refugeecouncil.org.uk/policy/responses/2005/women. htm accessed 20 .11.05

Rice, C., McGregor, N., Thomson, H. and Udagawa, C. (2004) *National English for Speakers of Other Languages (ESOL) Strategy: Mapping Exercise and Scoping Study*, Edinburgh: Scottish Executive
http://www.scotland.gov.uk/Resource/Doc/35596/0029540.pdf

Roberts, C., Baynham, M., Shrubshall, P., Barton, D., Chopra, P., Cooke, M., Hodge, R., Pitt, K., Schellekens, P., Wallace, C. and Whitfield, S. (2004), *English for Speakers of Other Languages (ESOL) – case studies of provision, learners' needs and resources*. London: NRDC.

Roberts, C. and Campbell, S. (2006) *Talk on Trial Job interviews, language and ethnicity*, Department for Work and Pensions Research report No 344.

Roberts, C., Davies, E. and Jupp, T. (1992) *Language and Discrimination*. London: Longman.

Roberts, C., Didley, N., Eldred, J., Brittan, J., Grief, S., Cooper, B., Baynham, M., Shrubshall, P., Windsor, V., Castellino, C and Walsh, M. (2005) *Embedded teaching and learning of adult literacy, numeracy and ESOL*. London: NRDC.

Robinson, D. and Reeve, K. (2006) *Neighbourhood experiences of new immigration: Reflections from the evidence base*. York: Joseph Rowntree Foundation.

Robinson, P. (1997) *Literacy, Numeracy and Economic Performance*. London: Centre for Economic Performance.

Rosenberg, S. (2006) 'NATECLA's role in the history of ESOL since 1986.' *Language Issues*, Vol. 18, No. 1: pp. 2–9.

Sagan, O. and Casey, H. (2005) 'Learners' first language in the classroom', *Reflect* Vol. 2, p. 23.

Schellekens, P. (2001) *English Language as a Barrier to Employment, Training and Education*. London: DfEE.

Schellekens, P. (2004) 'Individual Learning Plans: fit for purpose?' *Reflect*, Vol. 1, pp. 4–5.

Schuller, T., Preston, J., Hammond, C., Brassett-Grundy, A. and Bynner, J. (2004) *The Benefits of Learning*. London: RoutledgeFalmer.

Scottish Executive (2006) *A Consultation on an Adult ESOL Strategy for Scotland. Analysis of Responses*,
http://www.scotland.gov.uk/Resource/Doc/115477/0028630.pdf

SEU (2001) *A new Commitment to Neighbourhood Renewal*, National Strategy Action Plan. London: Social Exclusion Unit.

SEU (2004) *Tackling Social Exclusion: Taking stock and looking to the future – emerging findings, March 2004*. London: Social Exclusion Unit.

Shrubshall and Roberts (2005) 'Being a nurse and following new rules: institutional and professional discourses in a preparatory course for supervised practice for overseas nurses' in Roberts *et al.* (eds.) *Embedded teaching and learning of adult literacy, numeracy and ESOL.* London: NRDC.

Spiegel, M. and Sunderland, H. (2006) *Teaching basic literacy to ESOL learners.* London: LLU+.

Stanistreet, P. (2004) 'The most important tool you can have is wanting to understand'. *Adults Learning,* Vol. 15, No. 2, pp. 9 –11.

Sunderland, H., Klein, C., Savinson, R., and Partridge, T. (1997) *Dyslexia and the bilingual learner.* London: LLU+

Sunderland, H. (2006) Teacher Education, unpublished paper submitted to the NIACE ESOL Inquiry.

Sunderland H. and Taylor C. (2006) Citizenship Materials for ESOL Learners, unpublished paper submitted to the NIACE ESOL Inquiry.

Sunderland, H and Wilkins, M. (2004) 'ILPs in ESOL: theory, research and practice,' *Reflect,* Vol. 1, pp. 8–9.

Tackey N. D., Casebourne J., Aston J., Ritchie H., Sinclair A., Tyers C., Hurstfield J., Willison R., and Page R. (2006) *Barriers to Employment for Pakistanis and Bangladeshis in Britain,* DWP Research Report DWPRR 360. London: DWP.

Taylor, C. (2007) *ESOL and citizenship. A teachers' guide,* Leicester: NIACE.

Trade Union Congress (2003) *Overworked, underpaid and over here. Migrant workers in Britain.* London: TUC.

TUC/BSA, (2000) *Basic Skills are Union Business.* London: Basic Skills Agency.

Uden (2004) *Learning's not a crime.* Leicester: NIACE.

Vorhaus, J. (2006) *Four years on. NRDC 2005-6 Findings and messages for policy and practice.* London: NRDC.

Waddington, S. (2005) *Valuing skills and supporting integration.* Leicester: NIACE.

Walker E., Betts, D., Dominey, J. and Goulding, J. (2000) *Effective management of part time lecturers.* London: Further Education Development Agency.

Ward, J. with Edwards, J. (2002) *Learning journeys: learners' voices. Learners' views on progress and achievement in literacy and numeracy.* London: Learning and Skills Development Agency.

Ward, J. (2004) Liverpool, Blackburn, Wirral ESOL Pathfinder Project: final background information report: internal evaluation, (unpublished).

Weir, M. (2005) 'ILPs: a trivialisation of teaching and learning?' *Reflect*, Vol. 2, pp. 29–30.

Winder, R. (2005) *Bloody Foreigners*. London: Abacus.

Yai, D., Marbini. A. and Balimoria, R. (2005) *The forbidden workforce: asylum seekers, the employment concession and access to the UK labour market*. London: Refugee Council.

Yarnit, M., Darshan, S. and Zwart, R. (2005) *Understanding learning brokerage*. London: Learning and Skills Development Agency.

Zaronaite, D. and Tirzite, A. (2006) *The Dynamics of Migrant Labour in South Lincolnshire*, Lincolnshire: South Holland District Council. http://www.migrantworker.co.uk/docs/The%20Dynamics%20of%20 Migrant%20Labour%20in%20South%20Lincolnshire%20(2).pdf

Zetter, R. with Griffiths, D., Sigona, N., Flynn, D., Pasha, T. and Beynon, R. (2006) *Immigration, social cohesion and social capital*. York: Joseph Rowntree Foundation http:/www.jrf.org.uk/bookshop/

# Index